DATE			

WELFARE
Helping Hand or Trap?

Ann E. Weiss

—Issues in Focus—

ENSLOW PUBLISHERS, INC.

Bloy St. & Ramsey Ave.	P.O. Box 38
Box 777	Aldershot
Hillside, N.J. 07205	Hants GU12 6BP
U.S.A.	U.K.

Library of Congress Cataloging-in-Publication Data

Weiss, Ann E., 1943-
    Welfare: helping hand or trap?

    (Issues in focus)
    Bibliography: p.
    Includes index.
    Summary: Considers the development of welfare, how it affects those in the
system, and recent changes in welfare in the United States.
    1. Public welfare—United States—Juvenile literature. [1. Public welfare] I. Title.
II. Series: Issues in focus (Hillside, N. J.)

HV91.W465   1990   361.973   89-16843
ISBN 0-89490-169-9

Printed in the United States of America

10 9 8 7 6 5 4 3 2 1

ABK 4915

Contents

1

The Worlds of Welfare

For Miguel Gonzalez, age nine, and his ten year-old sister Kissey, the world centers around the home the two share with their mother Nancy. In 1987, that home was in the Prince George Hotel on Manhattan's East Twenty-eighth Street.

The address may sound elegant, but Miguel and Kissey know it is anything but. When they went to live there, the Prince George was one of several dozen New York City "welfare hotels." At one time, the hotels were stately buildings that offered temporary shelter to the rich, powerful, and famous, but by the late 1980s their deteriorating remnants were being used by the city as long-term emergency housing for thousands of needy men, women, and children who could afford nowhere else to live.

Welfare hotels in New York and elsewhere are squalid places. Trash and litter are all about. The air reeks with the stench of the filth piled in corridors and stairwells. The hotels can be dangerous places as well. Building violations may abound, and so may violations of health and housing codes. In 1986, the owner of one New York City welfare hotel had been cited by city officials for about a thousand separate violations. Often, such violations go uncorrected for months, even years, and city officials cannot be much surprised when fires break out in ancient hotel wiring, or when babies and toddlers fall from broken or unbarred windows high above the street level.

Other forms of danger lurk in the dark corridors and huge echoing public rooms of America's welfare hotels. Drunks sleep in hallways, sprawl on the steps, argue in loud voices. At the Prince George, Miguel and Kissey soon learned to take care to stay out of their way. Drug pushers, including those who deal in crack, the powerful and deadly form of cocaine, ply their trade openly inside the hotels or on the sidewalks in front of them.

Upstairs, in the single room the Gonzalezes called home, conditions were a little better. The children knew how lucky they were that their family was small; many of their friends and fellow tenants were living jammed six or seven to a room. And Nancy worked hard at making things as clean, decent, and safe as she could for her family. Her job wasn't easy, though, in one room with no privacy and few amenities—not even a place to prepare food or eat. The Gonzalezes could sleep in the room, but that was about all. Meals were eaten community-style at long tables in the hotel's former dining rooms. Typically, according to a report in *The New York Times,* the one hot meal of the day consisted of "breaded meat, pale mixed vegetables and a small cup of fruit."

Kissey and Miguel did find one means of escape from the Prince George: school. Their school—P.S. 151—was three miles away on East Ninety-first Street. It takes a long time to travel three miles in New York's rush-hour traffic, and each schoolday morning the two had to be at the bus stop before seven o'clock. To the 12,000 children living in New York City welfare hotels in 1987, school offered more than a physical escape from dirt and danger. It represented hope for the future. Miguel wants to be a lawyer or a policeman and Kissey, a doctor. "Both of them know they have to study hard," their mother told a reporter from *The New York Times,* "because, as Kissey said, she wants to make sure she isn't ever in this situation again." Who could blame her? For Kissey and her family, the world of welfare has proved to be a grim world indeed.

Other Welfare Concerns

Those who provide that world see it as grim, too, but in a different way. The dictionary defines "welfare" as "organized community or corporate efforts for social betterment of a class or group." In common usage, the word signifies governmental or private charitable programs aimed at making sure every individual has sufficient food, money, and other necessities upon which to live. Most Americans agree that government has a responsibility to help care for the needy, but the job is huge. In 1987, fifty more New York City families were entering welfare hotels each month than were moving out of them and into apartments of their own. And the welfare hotel population was only the tip of the welfare iceberg. Across the country, the total number of families considered "poor" according to federally established income figures went from just over 19 million in 1978 to over 33 million in 1985.

The welfare price tag has been rising, too. The bill for one program alone, Aid to Families with Dependent Children (AFDC), amounted to about $7 billion a year in 1973. Over the next eleven years, it more than doubled. It is ordinary wage-earning taxpayers who end up footing that bill. For many of them, the world of welfare seems a costly burden and is a cause of deep resentment.

Others involved in welfare have less reason to resent the system. Private landlords have done very well out of New York's welfare hotels. According to *The New York Times*, the hotel with the thousand violations in 1986—the Holland Hotel in midtown Manhattan—showed $3 million in profits that year.

Slumlords are not the only ones profiting from the nation's welfare systems, critics charge. In the late 1970s, a Maine woman named Donna Gilbeau created three false identities for herself, claiming a total of eleven children. Not only did she apply for and receive aid under AFDC, but she also obtained food stamps, issued by the U.S. Department of Agriculture, with which to buy groceries. In all, Gilbeau admitted, she cheated the state and federal governments out of over $70,000 during an eight-year period. Sentenced to ten years in prison, she expected to serve only a couple of years with time off for good behavior.

Gilbeau was not the first person to commit welfare fraud—nor will she be the last. No one knows how much government spends "supporting" nonexistent men, women, and children every year. Furthermore, many Americans are convinced that thousands of girls and women deliberately become pregnant for the express purpose of upping their AFDC payments. To people who believe that, the world of welfare is a place populated largely by cheats and chiselers.

Cheats and chiselers nothing! retort social workers and most other welfare professionals. The majority of welfare recipients are men, women, and children whose only "fault" is that they have, through circumstances beyond their control, lost a home, a job, a family—lost, perhaps, their way in life. Once on welfare, the professionals say, it's hard to get off. Welfare provides some temporary solutions, but few long-term ones. It may give someone a bed to sleep in, but permanent affordable housing is another matter entirely. Welfare may offer a free meal or food stamps, but it has not been a means to a good job, or even to job training or a basic education. What is more, advocates for America's welfare population continue, poverty worsened in the United states during the 1980s, and as the nation entered the final decade of the twentieth century, the welfare trap was deeper and more difficult than ever for those in it to escape.

Talking About Welfare

How do welfare recipients themselves feel about their world? Some, like Carol Sasaki, of Albany, New York, know welfare as a stepping stone that allowed them to move from a world of want to world of opportunity. As a thirteen-year-old, Carol ran away from home to crash in a San Francisco apartment with a striptease dancer and a number of Hell's Angels motorcyclists. Later, she moved to Seattle, had a son, and went on welfare. The social workers assigned to her case tried to place her in a low-paying unskilled job, but Carol resisted, refusing to leave her baby in what she considered to be less-than-adequate day care. Three times she tried—and failed—to pass a high school diploma equivalency exam. "I was considered hopeless," she says now.

She wasn't hopeless, though. One day she met a professional woman who told her that she herself had once been right where Carol was then, on welfare and apparently doomed to stay there. "That haunted me," Carol said later, "knowing someone who had made it." Carol decided that she was going to make it, too. Still on relief, she met her high school requirements and started attending classes at a community college. By 1987, she had her college B.A. and Master's degrees and was working toward a Ph.D. in international studies. For Carol Sasaki, the world of welfare had been a doorway to a bright new future.

Will welfare open doors for Miguel and Kissey Gonzalez? Sadly, the odds are against it. Too many children who grow up in welfare homes and hotels go on welfare themselves. "The majority [of these children] end up like their parents," warned Ernie Richardson, director of a New York after-school program aimed at helping those living in welfare hotels. "The little girls will be like their mothers—pregnant." The boys become uncontrollable in their early teens. For them, the world of welfare is a world they may never leave.

A grim, dead-end world . . . a pathway to success . . . a ripe ground for frauds and cheats . . . an obligation of government . . . a burden on the taxpayer . . . welfare in the United States is all of these, and more. How did the system get that way? Are systems different in other parts of the world? What is welfare's past? Its future?

2
The History of Welfare

Many ages ago, in the land of Egypt along the Nile River in north-eastern Africa, Pharaoh had a dream. It seemed to the king that he stood on the bank of a river and that out of the river came seven cattle, "fat fleshed and well favored." The cattle began grazing in a lush meadow. Then after them came seven other cattle, "poor and very ill favored," leaner than any Pharaoh had ever seen. The dream woke Pharaoh, but soon he slept and dreamed again.

Again, his vision had two parts. First, he saw seven plump-kerneled ears of corn, then seven thin, withered ones. What could the dream signify?

The Hebrew slave Joseph might know, Pharaoh's chief butler suggested. He had something of a reputation for interpreting dreams. Sure enough, Joseph was able to explain Pharaoh's vision. The seven fat cattle and the seven fat ears of corn meant there would be seven years of plentiful harvests. The seven lean cattle and the seven wasted ears meant that after the bounty would come seven years of famine. Take advantage of the seven fruitful years, Joseph advised Pharaoh, and put someone in charge of storing up corn and other foodstuffs against the bad times to follow. Pharaoh heeded Joseph's words and assigned to the Hebrew himself the task of gathering food for the future.

Egypt was not the only place where long-ago rulers sought to provide for their people's welfare. Another was the Rome of the second century B.C. In those days, Rome was a republic, a state in which citizens elect their leaders. When famine struck in about the middle of the century, the Roman government took on the job of feeding its population. Government agents began buying wheat in order to sell it to consumers at a fixed low price. No "means test" was imposed; that is, people did not have to prove that they were poor or in need in order to line up and await their turn to buy. Anyone who wanted the wheat might have it at the subsidized rate. About 50,000 Romans took advantage of this program, which was supported by contributions from the rich as well as through taxes.

The Roman wheat subsidy continued for generations. And it grew. When Julius Caesar marched into the city and effectively transformed the republic into an empire in 49 B.C., it was serving about 320,000 citizens. By imposing a means test, Caeser cut that figure to 150,000 of the most destitute. Slowly, however, the number showing up on the "bread line" rose again, reaching over 300,000 during the reign of Julius Caesar's nephew, the emperor Augustus. A new means test ordered by Augustus reduced that by about a third, and the relief rolls stayed more or less at that level for the next three hundred years. By then, recipients were getting pork, olive oil, and salt, as well as wheat or bread.

This system of relief did more than feed Rome's poor. It helped maintain the peace. Rome's early emperors were a high-living, big-spending lot, and the luxurious lifestyle they and other wealthy Romans enjoyed contrasted sharply with the wretched living conditions of the city's poor. The emperors relied upon the dole to keep the neediest and hungriest content enough to prevent them from erupting into rioting or outright rebellion. At the same time, the emperors took care to provide Romans with food for the spirit. Lavish entertainments—bloody contests between professional gladiators or fighters, battles that pitted men against wild animals, and the public torture and execution of members of the new Christian church—were staged to

11

amuse the crowds and divert public attention from the miseries of everyday life in Rome's slums. "Bread and circuses" is the phrase used to describe this particular Roman social policy.

Poverty in the Middle Ages

In the fifth century A.D. the Roman Empire came under fierce attack from Huns, Goths, Visigoths, and other tribesmen of eastern Europe and Asia. As the barbarians pushed further and further west and south through France and onto the Italian peninsula, the empire and its government fell. The Dark Ages of medieval Europe had begun.

During those ages, which lasted for about eight hundred years, governments did little if anything about the welfare needs of their people. What relief programs there were in Europe rested in the hands of the Roman Catholic Church.

That was appropriate, since the Church was of God and it was God, people believed, who was responsible for poverty in the world. It was God, after all, who decreed that one man should be a prince and another a peasant. It was God who determined who should be rich and who must live in want. It was God who sent the droughts and floods that ruined crops and the famines that left people to starve. God had decreed that poverty should exist, and there was nothing any human being could do to rid the earth of it. There was nothing the poor could do about their poverty, either. It was hopeless for them to complain about it or to think they could ever climb out of it. Hadn't Jesus himself told his disciples, "Ye have the poor always with you?" Poverty would always be around, and it was up to God's Church to deal with its human effects.

Responding to the need, churches and religious groups throughout Europe established hospitals, orphanages, and poorhouses to shelter the homeless. Many were located in monasteries and run by monks. Charitable institutions might also be set up by wealthy individuals or members of merchants' associations or craft guilds.

The assumptions of the Middle Ages—that poverty is inevitable and not the fault of the poor themselves—held sway in Europe for hundreds of years. Then, in 1347, something happened to change everything.

Plague—and Change

In October of that year, a group of trading ships fresh from a voyage through the Black Sea put into harbor in Sicily. They carried a terrible cargo: a load of sailors dead or dying of a disease thought to have originated in China. That disease was the bubonic plague.

Within three years, the plague had swept across all of Europe. No one can say for sure how many perished during that first epidemic. According to the French chronicler Jean Froissart, who witnessed the scourge at first hand, "a third of the world died." Modern scholars, like the American historian Barbara Tuchman, accept this as a fair estimate.

Any disaster of such magnitude is bound to have profound effects upon society. In the case of the plague, one effect was the breakup of the social structure of medieval Europe. Another was a far-reaching change in its economy.

Before the plague, European social structure was as it had been since the onset of the Dark Ages. It was a structure set by custom and, most people believed, by God. Priests, bishops, and other members of the clergy were ordained to intercede with heaven on behalf of the laiety. The nobility was on earth to rule and to command armies. Then there were the knights and yeomen who served in those armies and a small middle class of traders, merchants, and craftsmen. And there was the peasantry, the vast majority of men and women whose harsh destiny it was to labor on the land of some lord or noble, to till his fields and care for his livestock, to harvest his crops and pay taxes. In return for their work, peasants were allowed to farm small plots or to share in part of the lord's harvest.

Although some peasants were free, and a few owned the huts they lived in and a small bit of land, most were serfs. Serfs were like slaves—with one difference. Slaves are regarded simply as pieces of property and "belong" directly to another. Medieval serfs did not belong to their lord as much as they did to the lord's land. If the lord died, or gave up his estate, or forfeited it to the king, he gave up his serfs at the same time. They went, with the land, to the lord's heir or to whoever else took over the estate.

With the plague, this system began breaking down. The death of one-third of the population meant, among other things, a lack of people to do all the jobs that needed doing. The labor shortage gave the peasant a measure of power. The few peasants who survived on an estate could demand higher compensation, usually in the form of more food or better living conditions, for their work. Some found that if they could get to a part of the country where laborers were in especially short supply, they could earn even more. Of course, serfs were forbidden by law to leave the land on which they were born, but in the confusion of the first plague years and during the smaller epidemics that followed, escaping became easier and more common. Some of the escapees found employment but others, unable or unwilling to work at the jobs offered, wandered around the countryside as vagrants. Some in this second group turned to thievery or petty crimes to support themselves.

The social and economic changes of the second half of the fourteenth century led to changes in people's basic assumptions about poverty and how to cope with it. In the stable world before the plague, everyone agreed that poverty came from God and that religious charity was the way to deal with it. But in the tumultuous new world of change and uncertainty, this comfortable assumption seemed unreasonable. People could improve their way of life, the peasants were learning. They need not remain poor if they could force employers to meet their wage demands, or if they moved to a place with more jobs. To the poor, it began to appear that their poverty was the result not of the will of God but of human customs and man-made laws. If those customs and laws were altered there might be an end to their poverty. Rumblings of discontent and demands for change began to be heard across Europe.

In a few places, including England, the demands burst into open revolt. June 1381 saw a ragtag collection of angry peasants from the southeastern part of the country begin a march on London. It was a violent group; the peasants seized the Tower of London, looted and burned a magnificent royal palace, and murdered several people. The king's men reacted quickly, and by the middle of the month, the rebellion had been brutally put down.

But even with the uprising crushed, the memory of it haunted the rich and powerful. At the same time, English leaders were disturbed by the problems of vagrancy and crime in the countryside and by rapidly rising wages in towns and cities. This combination of concerns led them to change certain of their own ideas. No longer could they assume it was safe to leave it up to the Church to deal with poverty. Charitable handouts were not going to be enough to satisfy angry mobs or keep ambitious men from seeking better pay and working conditions. Like the emperors of ancient Rome, England's king and the nobles, barons, and knights who made up its Parliament decided to take matters into their own hands and turn to a form of public relief to appease the poor. But the king and Parliament did not intend to quell dissent with a haphazard program of bread and circuses. Instead, in 1388, the country adopted a Poor Law Act.

English Poor Law

The law's primary aim was to put a lid on the growing economic power of the lower class by fixing wages at firm and unalterable levels. Not only would fixed wages save money for employers, but they would also make running away pointless for the peasantry. With wages the same everywhere, there would be no sense in people roaming about trying to better themselves. In addition, the law placed direct restrictions on travel by outlawing vagrancy.

The new law was not a great success. Forbidding vagrancy is not the same as stopping it, and people who were discontented in one part of England went right on looking for better opportunities, or better luck, in other parts. Vagrancy actually grew over the next century and a half. Nor did the fixed-wage provision of the law prove enforceable. By 1536, during the reign of King Henry VIII, it was clear that a new poor law was needed.

Parliament's 1536 law, like its 1388 measure, represented an effort to crack down on vagrancy and crime and end social unrest. It, too, attempted to deal with poverty by suppressing the poor. Yet it differed from the earlier act in one striking way. It distinguished between two groups of the poor: those whose misfortune truly seemed sent by God and those whose poverty appeared to stem from shiftlessness or bad habits. To the people in the first group—the blind, the crippled, the sick, the very old, the very young—Parliament promised some relief. Taxes would be collected to pay for the support of these "impotent poor." Government would assume no responsibility for members of the second group, though. The "able-bodied poor," people who were healthy but who did not or would not find jobs, were to be punished. In 1547, Parliament set that punishment as a period of enslavement.

Over the years, the separation of the needy into the impotent and the able-bodied—into the deserving or "good" poor as opposed to the undeserving or "bad" poor—became more and more deeply entrenched in English law. Between 1558 and 1601, Parliament enacted three major poor laws, each based on the idea of such a separation. The first had the goal of "setting the poor on work." The other two similarly tied relief to willingness to find a job. Together, the measures divided the poor into three classes: the impotent, the able-bodied who seemed unable to win employment, and the able-bodied who refused to work or who persisted in vagrancy. The first were to be maintained in a poorhouse or almshouse at public expense. The second were placed in "houses of industry," or workhouses, and assigned to perform such tasks as spinning flax or wool, sewing and weaving, and blacksmithing. The third faced punishment: a whipping or having the letter *V*—for Vagrant—burned into the skin with a red-hot branding iron.

Cruel as their penalties were, these new poor laws had some merits. For one thing, they established the idea (an idea not always carried out in practice) that the community as a whole had a duty to provide care for those of its members most clearly unable to help themselves. For another, they made providing that care a matter of local responsibility. Every town or parish had to support its own needy, which meant taxpayers were looking out for neighbors and fellow townspeople rather than paying for the upkeep of strangers. Local administrators, knowledgeable about local conditions and the specific needs of their own poor, were appointed to manage each parish's welfare program.

But the laws had their weaknesses as well. Making local taxpayers support their own impotent poor led to rivalry among parishes. If a man moved from one parish to another, and then to still another and went on relief, which parish had to pay? If a woman left her home to marry and then came back an indigent widow, whose burden was she? Arguments among parishes anxious to reduce their welfare bills were fierce. Eventually, the Settlement Act of 1662 linked legal residency firmly to birth, marriage, and apprenticeship. (An apprentice is someone who trains for a skilled job while working at low wages or without pay for whoever provides the training.) The Settlement Act helped resolve quarrels among England's parishes, although it hardly ended them altogether.

There were other problems with these poor laws. They never stopped vagrancy, for example, any more than the 1388 statute had. Since the end of the fourteenth century, English society had become more mobile, not less. Furthermore, the country's economy continued to change. The change was particularly apparent by the early 1500s, as English explorers and adventurers in the New World began sending shiploads of precious metals back home. The new wealth helped cause inflation—a sharp rise in prices—making it harder and harder for the poor to afford the necessities of daily living.

The third problem with the poor laws stemmed from the fact that the labor shortages of the plague years were now a thing of the past.

England's population was rising—from about two and a half million at the start of the sixteenth century to approximately four million a hundred years later and to six million a century after that. More people meant more competition for jobs that were increasingly hard to find. Greater mobility, inflation, and joblessness conspired to deepen the welfare dilemma and to heat up public resentment over its cost. Other problems in the system had to do with workhouse conditions. The infant death rate in the country's parish workhouses stood at an appalling 59 percent as the year 1700 approached. By the middle of the eighteenth century, the country's welfare system was in deep crisis, and within fifty years it was falling apart under a series of new strains.

One strain flowed from England's penchant for going to war. There was war against France from 1756 to 1763, and only a little more than a decade after that fighting ended, the country found itself engaged in an unsuccessful struggle to keep its American colonies from winning independence. As usual, the wars created impoverished widows and orphans, caused inflation, and drained the country of the resources needed by its civilian population. Another strain was the famine that followed five years of bad harvests in the 1790s. Severest of all the strains on English relief, though, were those that stemmed from the Industrial Revolution.

The Industrial Revolution

The Industrial Revolution, which began in the middle of the eighteenth century and lasted approximately a hundred years, was a period of rapid scientific, technical, and economic change. Like the changes of the fourteenth-century plague years, they brought social changes, and shifts in people's ideas and assumptions as well.

It was the steam engine that powered the Industrial Revolution, and the model patented by inventor James Watt in 1769 transformed England almost overnight. Steam engines worked with an efficiency utterly foreign to wind or water power. Suddenly it was possible for huge machines to turn out goods in greater numbers and at faster speeds than most people had ever dreamed of. And there were other kinds of scientific and technological changes. The telegraph speeded communications. Trains pulled by powerful new steam locomotives, together with miles of newly laid track, did the same for transportation.

The technical changes led to social and economic ones. Following jobs from countryside to town, thousands of men and women uprooted themselves from their rural homes and moved into crowded cities. There, lifestyles changed dramatically. Before moving, the cottage weaver had set his own hours and turned out as much good work in a day as he could. The village blacksmith, its miller, its potter, and its seamstress had done the same, and all were paid accordingly. All lived and worked much as their parents, grandparents, and great-grandparents had done, often in the very homes of those forebears. Custom and tradition governed the rhythms of their lives.

In the factory, there was no custom and no tradition, and the rhythm was the rhythm of the machinery, of pounding pistons and fast-moving parts. Workers were expected to keep up with that rhythm for as much as ten or twelve hours a day. What they earned was set, not by themselves and the amount and quality of the work they performed, but by the factory owner, who was naturally eager to extract the greatest amount of labor for the lowest possible wages—often only a few pennies a day.

The low pay condemned factory hands to life in the meanest and most dismal areas of the city, slums in which poor nutrition and a lack of sanitation guaranteed illness and epidemics. In the manufacturing town of Manchester, 12 percent of working-class families were living in cellars in 1840. The brutal conditions under which people worked exhausted them and further damaged their health. Exhaustion also led to on-the-job accidents, and factory deaths were not uncommon, especially among children. The sick and injured received little help or sympathy from their employers, or from government. Thrown out of work, they were replaced by new able-bodied arrivals in England's burgeoning cities.

Where did the unemployed go then? Some returned to the country, knowing there was little chance of finding work there. Still, the parish of their birth, marriage, or apprenticeship was obliged to take them in and give them a place in the poorhouse or the workhouse. Or the unemployed might elect to stay in the city, eking out an existence with part-time employment, putting their children to work, even by begging or stealing.

Of course the misery of slum and factory was only one side of the coin in England and other industrialized nations. For the people in those countries who owned factories, or who had enough capital—money—to set up a successful enterprise or to invest in one, the opportunities seemed boundless in the last half of the eighteenth century and the first half of the nineteenth. Hundreds of such capitalists became enormously wealthy during that time. Even many who had started out with almost nothing at all found themselves climbing into the ranks of the well-to-do. The industrialized world was seeing its first "self-made" men.

In the public eye, and in their own view as well, the self-made seemed to share a number of personal qualities. Chief among them were ambition, determination, a shrewd business sense and most important, a willingness to work hard. It wasn't long before the idea took hold that anyone possessing those excellent qualities could get rich.

Along with that idea went another: people who fail to prosper—who are unable to earn even enough to support themselves and their families—fail because they are unambitious, lacking determination and know-how, and, above all, lazy. The poor, in other words, are poor because of the kind of human beings they are. They have only themselves to blame for their condition. Not only that, the poor enjoy their poverty. They like being on relief.

And why shouldn't they? wealthy Europeans asked. Look at the way public relief allowed them to live. By the end of the eighteenth century, the country's parish poorhouses had grown so crowded that many of the needy were being offered "outdoor" relief. Outdoor meant outside the poorhouse. People on outdoor relief stayed in their own homes and received regular allowances of food or cash. Even the employed could get such an allowance if their wages fell below the subsistence level regarded as necessary for survival. Besides that, a separate allowance might be offered for each child in a poor family.

The results of such a system should have been obvious from the start, critics contended. Under it, the poor had no incentive to try to better their lot through honest labor. In fact, they had every incentive to let it worsen. Hard-working or lazy, it didn't matter. Society would take care of those who couldn't be bothered taking care of themselves. Outdoor relief also gave the poor every reason to produce one child after another—and to let the parish pay the bill, the critics charged, adding that the system afforded special encouragement to unmarried mothers. "To the woman, a single illegitimate child is seldom any expense," one outraged citizen wrote, "and two or three are a source of positive profit." The point is highly debatable, but many accepted it then, just as today some Americans believe women become pregnant in order to qualify for welfare.

The profit—if any—came at the expense of the taxpayer. In 1785, England's 15,000 parishes were spending about £2 million a year on welfare. By about 1820, the figure had risen to nearly £8 million. Eight million pounds a year was a terrible amount for society to pay for poverty, people said—especially if one assumed that the poverty was the poor's own fault.

The Poor Law Commission and the Workhouse System

In 1832, Parliament appointed a Poor Law Commission to look into the country's welfare system and recommend changes. The commissioners were convinced even before they began their work that the poor must be blamed for their condition and that relief allowances increase dependency. The report they issued two years later faithfully reflected those biases. The plan it proposed was called the workhouse system, but the kind of workhouses the commissioners envisioned bore little resemblance to the workhouses of the last half of the

21

sixteenth century. Those workhouses, however unsuccessful they may have been in the long run, were founded upon the assumption that society has some obligation toward its poor. The new system represented a movement away from that assumption. Its workhouses were deliberately designed to be harsh enough to keep all but the most abjectly poor from even applying to them for shelter.

"The first and most essential of all conditions [for a person on relief] . . . is that his situation . . . shall not be made really or apparently so eligible [by 'eligible' commission members meant 'desirable'] as the situation of the independent laborer of the lowest class," the report concluded. It listed three ways that workhouse life might be made just about intolerable.

"First, by giving to the pauper . . . worse food, worse clothing, and worse lodging than he could have obtained by the average wages of his labor . . . " This became known as the principle of "less eligibility."

"Second . . . to require from the applicant for relief, toil more severe or more irksome than that endured by the independent laborer . . . " That was the dogma of the "workhouse test." To receive aid, applicants had to prove themselves willing to perform such toil.

"The third . . . is to require [the recipient] . . . to enter an abode provided for him by the public, where . . . excitement and mere amusement are excluded—an abode where he is . . . deprived of beer, tobacco, and spirits—is . . . separated from his usual associates and his usual pastimes . . .

"This is the workhouse system. "

The same year the Poor Law Commission submitted its report, Parliament enacted the Poor Law Amendment Act of 1834. The new law embodied the commission report in its entirety—workhouses, workhouse test, and principle of less eligibility. From then on in England, individual parishes were no longer responsible for their own poor. Relief was centralized, directed on a nationwide basis. For the remainder of the century, the dreaded shadow of the workhouse loomed over Britain's poor.

The typical nineteenth-century English workhouse was a grim jail-like two-story building of dingy red brick. Most were constructed around open dirt courtyards. Inside, forty cots might be crammed into a single, frequently filthy dormitory room. Families were separated upon entering the workhouse. Many workhouse children had no parents or lived apart from them. One, an illegitimate boy named John Rowlands, was placed in a workhouse by his foster family in 1847. John later changed his name to Henry Morton Stanley. He was to win fame—and an eventual knighthood—as the newspaperman who located the missing English explorer David Livingstone in the heart of Africa in 1871. Stanley's greeting, "Dr. Livingstone, I presume?" is legendary.

As an adult, Stanley wrote movingly of his life in the workhouse between his sixth and fifteenth years. His half sister, like him labeled "a deserted bastard," was housed in the same institution, but though he sometimes spotted her at a distance, he was never allowed to speak to her. When his own mother came to visit him the year he was twelve, the boy was astounded. He had not realized that workhouse children had parents.

The manner in which nineteenth-century English society punished young John Rowlands for being a penniless orphan was cruel indeed. Like his fellow inmates, John was roused by a bell at six each morning and locked in his dormitory at eight every evening. Meals revolved around bread, rice, potatoes, and gruel, a thin flour-and-water porridge. The children wore uniforms of a cheap, sleazy material and the boys' hair was "mown close to the skull."

True to its name, the workhouse system required those condemned to it to work. Fifty years after the fact, Stanley vividly remembered "sweeping the playground with brooms more suited to giants than little children . . . washing the slated floors when one was stiff from caning . . . hoeing . . . frost-bound ground." For adults, the labor was more onerous still: a typical task was crushing animal bones into powder for use as fertilizer. Those assigned to this job might be locked into a room eight feet wide and fourteen feet long and forced to work there seven hours a day.

The canings, or beatings, suffered by John Rowlands came at the hands of James Francis, the workhouse schoolmaster. Francis taught the boys out of the Bible, the catechism of the Church of England, and a fifty-year-old spelling book. (Girls were lucky to receive even that degree of academic instruction. Their "education" was limited to housekeeping matters.) Of the two worst beatings Stanley recalled, one came when he was eight—he had mispronounced the name "Joseph" in class—and the other when, at age ten, he broke a workhouse rule by eating some wild blackberries.

When he was fifteen, John Rowlands escaped from the workhouse. Schoolmaster Francis had found a few scratches on a table, and he furiously promised to cane every boy in the place in retaliation. Possibly thinking of the grisly discovery he and some of the others had made earlier—they had come upon a classmate's bloody, beaten body in the institution's mortuary—John determined not to submit to one more flogging. He knocked Francis to the ground, thrashed him soundly, and fled. Francis was not punished for the brutal murder although he did die in another harsh type of nineteenth-century English public institution—an insane asylum.

Naturally, conditions were not as bad as this in all English workhouses. In some, they were worse.

Gradually, however, over the course of the century, those conditions lightened. In 1891, workhouse children were allowed toys and books. The next year, men won the right to use tobacco. The changes may have been slight, but they must have been welcome.

Social Reform and the Welfare State

Other late nineteenth-century welfare reforms were more significant. Once again, the reforms were in large part a response on the part of government to threats of social unrest, threats that had erupted into widespread violence some years earlier, in 1848. At the same time, they reflected some new assumptions about the nature and causes of poverty.

By the late 1800s, the Industrial Revolution was about over. Although more technological advances were to come and still are coming a century later, Europe had completed its fundamental switch from a rural farming economy to an urban factory one. As before, social and economic changes meant changes in people's attitudes.

Back in 1832, with the Industrial Revolution in full swing, it had been relatively easy for English society to convince itself that anyone with a little gumption and a desire to work can get ahead and that those who are poor are that way only because their characters are flawed. Fifty years later, though, it was becoming apparent that industriousness is not the only key to success, and that people might fail through no fault of their own. It was clear, for instance, that economies operate in cycles—some years are good and others are bad. In the good years, business booms, people have money and they are willing to spend it on a wide range of goods. Factories hum, and more and more workers are hired. Their wages rise and poverty declines.

Then for some reason come the bad times. Perhaps inflation makes it difficult for people to buy the manufactured goods they want. Factory owners cut production and lay off workers. Unemployment rises, and so does poverty. It's not that workers don't want jobs—the jobs just aren't there.

Understanding the basic facts about how a modern economy operates and accepting the idea that the poor may not, after all, be to blame for their condition led to demands for changes in welfare legislation. The demands were heard, not just in England, but in other countries as well, and the changes came first in Germany. Between 1883 and 1887, that country's Reichstag—its law-making body—enacted legislation that radically altered the relationship between government and the poor and became a model for reform efforts throughout the industrialized world. Basic to the new system was a scheme of national insurance for disabled, ill, and retired workers. The insurance was compulsory; all workers were required to participate. Their wages were taxed, and the money collected was put in a special fund to be disbursed as necessary.

Austria copied Germany's national insurance plan in 1888, and Hungary adopted a similar system three years later. England, which had only gotten as far as supplying workhouse children with reading matter and playthings by 1891, did its copying in stages. The year 1908 saw passage of the Old Age Pensions Act and 1911 of the National Insurance Act, which provided some, but not all, industrial workers with sickness and unemployment benefits. Widows and orphans were granted aid in 1925, and seven years later, unemployment insurance coverage was extended to greater numbers of workers.

Finally, in 1948, three years after World War II ended, Parliament enacted a complete system of cradle-to-grave welfare security. After that, England rated along with the Scandinavian nations as one of the world's leading "welfare states." The British National Health Service became particularly comprehensive, offering free medical care to everyone in the land. By the late 1980s, that service was costing British taxpayers $41 billion a year. In a welfare state like England's or Sweden's, taxes can take up to 50 percent of the average worker's income.

Meantime, what of the United States? How was it coping with the welfare needs of its people? Or did any such need exist?

3

Welfare in the United States

The U.S. government did *not* need to develop programs of public relief, American lawmakers agreed. The agreement reflected attitudes that had been almost three hundred years in the making.

It all began back in the early 1600s with people like Edward and Sarah Pool. Edward had been born in the small English coastal town of Weymouth in 1609. The young Pools were hard working and ambitious, but they were far from rich, and it seemed to them that their chances of bettering themselves in their native land were small. And so, in 1635, the two made up their minds to emigrate to America and try their luck there, in the Massachusetts Bay Colony.

But how would they get to America? Edward and Sarah had no money and no way to pay for their passage across the ocean. So Edward resolved to indenture himself to one George Allen, a well-to-do acquaintance who was also headed for the colonies. Allen paid the couple's fare and Edward signed a contract that bound him to work for Allen—without pay—for two or three years. At the end of that time, he would have discharged his debt and be free to seek his fortune.

All went as the Pools had hoped. They reached Massachusetts safely. Edward served out his indenture and, in the process of finding a home for himself and Sarah, helped establish the town he called

27

Weymouth, a few miles south of Boston. When Edward Pool died in 1664, his will listed seven children as heirs. The seven shared a sizable estate, for in his thirty-odd years in the New World, Edward had become a wealthy man. He had made the long journey from indentured servant to master of a substantial property, from poverty to prosperity.

A Land of Opportunity

His success story was to be repeated over and over in America during the next three centuries. Other new arrivals discovered the same rich farmland and the same uncut forests that had greeted the Pools. The land seemed to be simply waiting for the settlers' plows and harrows and the woods for their axes. Game was abundant, and valuable fur-bearing creatures roamed the wilderness as well. Lakes, streams, and rivers teemed with fish, and to the west stretched endless plains and grasslands capable of supporting huge herds of meat and dairy animals.

All these resources belonged to anyone who could seize them and put them to use. Even the land itself went to whoever managed to establish a claim on it. Early successful claimants to much of what is now the eastern United States included the kings of England, and from time to time, those kings gave parts of their holdings away. In 1664, for instance, Charles II signed over the entire area between the Connecticut and Delaware rivers to his brother James, Duke of York. In addition, James received Nantucket Island, Martha's Vineyard, eastern Maine, and the present state of New York. Later, Charles repaid a debt to the Quaker William Penn with a grant of over 40,000 square miles of territory.

The lucky recipients of the king's bounty were openhanded in their turn. Penn dubbed his windfall "Pennsylvania"—Penn's Woods—and divided much of it up among English Quakers eager to escape religious persecution in their homeland. The Duke of York parceled out land in his territories as well or sold it at bargain rates. In later years, trappers, traders, and farmers pushed further westward into the frontier country of Kentucky, Tennessee, and Ohio, staking their claims to free or low-cost land there.

The giveaways continued long after the American colonists had fought for and won their independence from England. In 1803, the U.S. government paid France $15 million for the Louisiana Purchase—all the land from the Mississippi River west to the Rocky Mountains and from the Gulf of Mexico on the south to the Canadian border on the north. Subsequently and in various other ways, the United States acquired Texas and a good chunk of Mexico, the Rocky Mountains as far north as Canada, California, the Pacific Northwest, Alaska, Hawaii, and more. Throughout the nineteenth century, the federal government gave large portions of these lands on a first-come, first-served basis to anyone who asked. Even today, the U.S. government sells and leases public land cheaply to ranchers, oil developers, lumberers, and others.

America possessed resources beyond the land itself, people realized as the Industrial Revolution got underway and gained momentum. Coal from Pennsylvania and West Virginia, the oil of Texas and Louisiana, the rich iron ore deposits around Lake Superior—all contributed to fueling that revolution. The men who gained control of these resources and their production, oilmen such as John D. Rockefeller and steel magnates like Andrew Carnegie and Henry Clay Frick, began amassing great fortunes.

But captains of industry were not the only ones to profit from America's tremendous natural wealth. Hundreds of thousands of European immigrants, many of whom arrived in this country as empty-handed as Edward and Sarah Pool had been in 1635, benefited, too. Most of the new arrivals were refugees from the ravages of the Industrial Revolution, men and women escaping malodorous streets and dismal factories, fleeing crowded tenements and deserted farms, running away from poverty and unemployment and the menace of the workhouse.

True, escape did not come easily, and the conditions many of them endured during their first years in the New World were as harsh as anything the Old World had to offer. American slums could be as terrible as European ones, sickness as rampant, misery as real. The United States had its almshouses as England had its poorhouses. Likewise, the jobs immigrants found waiting for them in coal mines, steel mills, ore smelters, and factories were likely to be ill-paid, dangerous, health-threatening, and menial. But at least the jobs existed. And in America people found something else that was less common in Europe: optimism and the belief that life would soon improve.

In general, the optimism was well founded. Immigrants might start out working long hours at dirty or disagreeable jobs, but most could count on moving up to something better eventually—or at least on seeing their sons and daughters do so. Slum life might be miserable, but families fed up with the big cities of the East could move west, into those immense, still almost empty lands, and set up in farming or ranching. If that didn't work out, they could go on to the booming new towns of the Pacific Coast. A man by himself could drift south onto the rangeland and find work as a cowboy or seek adventure panning for gold in California or Alaska. There were business opportunities as well. Anyone who managed to accumulate a little capital could invest it and hope to become rich that way. The options seemed limitless in this great land of opportunity, and out of that wealth of possibilities there emerged the idea of the American Dream—the belief that anyone—anyone at all, no matter how poor, unfortunate, or disadvantaged—can succeed in life merely by grabbing whatever opportunity comes along and working hard at it.

The Idea of the American Dream

In itself, of course, this idea was very similar to the theories so dear to the hearts of men like the English public servants who dreamed up that nation's workhouse system in the early 1800s. They, too, believed that success is the reward of industriousness. And they, like their American counterparts, believed the reverse as well—that poverty results from laziness and bad character and that the poor are responsible for their own lot. But as we saw in the last chapter, European ideas changed during the nineteenth century, and by the late 1800s, people in countries like England and Germany had largely abandoned this blame-the-poor way of thinking. People in the United States had not.

Why? Because the European experience over the course of the Industrial Revolution had been so different from the American. By the end of the nineteenth century, people on both sides of the Atlantic were realizing that industrialization has its drawbacks as well as its advantages. For instance, Americans learned, as Europeans had, that business moves in cycles. But when bad times came in Europe, people couldn't simply pull up stakes and head for new frontiers. Europe had no frontier. Another essential difference between Europe and the United States was that many of Europe's natural resources had been depleted through centuries of use. The shortage of resources made it harder and harder for Europe to support its entire population. America's abundance, on the other hand, showed little sign of running out.

The material differences between Europe and the United States went a long way toward explaining the difference in public attitudes. Shortages and a want of options forced Europeans to consider the possibility that a lack of success may have as much to do with a lack of opportunity as with a lack of diligence. As citizens in a land of plenty, Americans could avoid facing that possibility. Europeans had solid evidence that how well people do in life is determined not by themselves alone but also by outside forces over which they have little or no control. Americans tended to overlook that aspect of the situation. Finally, Europeans had reason to suspect that whether people succeed or fail has less to do with the kind of people they are than with the kind of social, political, and economic conditions under which they are forced to live. Having a low income may not be the result of a person's unwillingness to work, but of a boss's unwillingness to raise

31

wages. Nor is joblessness always due to laziness. Sometimes it is due to a war or a factory shutdown or a business failure. Americans, blessed with a wealth of personal opportunity—free land, a richness of resources, and plenty of jobs—were less quick to recognize the part that society may play in creating poverty.

So while Americans clung to the idea that poverty is an individual matter and that each poor person must be considered responsible for himself or herself, Europeans were switching to the conviction that any capitalist society will always have a certain number of poor people. Capitalism requires a degree of poverty, they thought, and even in the best of times, some men and women must remain unemployed.

Why? In order for business to grow and expand—and growth and expansion are what capitalism is all about—there must be a pool of workers who want jobs. But if everyone already has a job, no such pool will be available. So if capitalism is to function properly, some people must be poor and out of work. And if people are poor because of the type of society they live in, European liberals argued, then it is up to that society to intervene and do what it can to help them. Thus it was that at the precise time Americans were most entranced by the idea of the American Dream, Europeans began taking their first tentative steps down the road toward the welfare state. It was a road, most Americans still thought, upon which it would never be necessary for this country to set foot.

Welfare—a Socialist Threat?

Not only were European-style welfare programs not needed in the United States, their American critics added, but implementing them here would be downright dangerous. Such programs were tainted by socialism. Who, after all, had been first to urge reform in Europe? Just to call them "liberals" was not enough. They were liberals, yes, but many of them were liberals with socialist ideas. In capitalist eyes, the merest hint of socialism seems a terrible thing.

Capitalism's objection to socialism is that the latter calls for public

32

ownership and control of business and industry. Socialists believe that a nation's means of production—its factories, mines, mills, and the like—should be taken away from their private owners and put in the hands of government managers. However, not all socialist programs are the same. Much of present-day Western Europe is socialized to the extent that a number of its major industries and utilities, such as transportation, communication, and the production of electricity, are owned and run by government. Hundreds of other money-making enterprises, though—supermarkets, department stores, hotels, apartment complexes, and so on—belong to individual capitalists. The Soviet Union and the nations of Eastern Europe have traditionally practiced a more extreme form of socialism. In most of these countries, the government has owned and operated virtually every business.

Not unnaturally, capitalists regard any degree of socialism as unfair. Taking industry away from its private owners, they say, amounts to stealing what people have created through their own hard work and ambition and punishing the very individuals in a society who have shown the most initiative. And it was individual initiative and the spirit of free enterprise that built this country. Take those away—as capitalists claim socialism would do—and America as we know it will be no more.

Besides rejecting national public welfare on the general grounds that it was socialistic, many nineteenth century Americans maintained that it harms those who receive it more than it helps them. How? A man's labor, his willingness and ability to work, is his own, just as surely as an industrialist's factory is *his* own. If government offers a poor man welfare, it deprives him of the necessity of working as hard as he can in order to support himself and his family. It takes away his need—which for a free human being is a right—to sell his labor in exchange for wages. With that loss, he also loses his individuality and his sense of initiative; his very independence is gone. So socialistic programs of public welfare would rob the poor as well as the rich.

Combined, the arguments had considerable force, and not for decades would the federal government become involved in welfare.

American Relief Systems

In the meantime, when and where public relief was needed, it was left up to state and local officials to provide it. Relief was needed, too, however much Americans might assure themselves to the contrary. For although the American Dream could, and often did, come true for people, the idea that the United States was the land of opportunity for all—the place where anyone with a little get-up-and-go and a willingness to work hard could succeed—was never more than a myth.

Behind the myth was stark reality. It was reality, for instance, that until well into the twentieth century, American women had few personal, property, or political rights and scant likelihood of ever making the dream come true for themselves. Black Americans had even less chance of success. Until the Civil War ended in 1865, nearly all of them were slaves with no legal or civil rights at all. Even after slavery was abolished, few blacks were permitted to vote or given decent schooling or job opportunities. Few blacks ever benefited from land giveaway programs. Members of other racial and ethnic groups also suffered political and economic discrimination in the United States. Even for those in a position to attain the dream, accomplishing it might take years of struggle. During that struggle, poverty was real and terrible.

By the early 1900s, a number of states were requiring cities and countries to offer some assistance to their neediest. Most of the aid went to those who would earlier have been called the impotent poor: the blind, elderly, and orphaned. Such individuals might receive grants of food, money or clothing. Any who were homeless could be boarded at public expense in private homes around town. Most local communities had to pay their own welfare costs, as only a few states went so far as to help defray expenses. Fortunately for those towns that did not get state reimbursement, welfare costs were rather easy to keep down. In the first place, the few programs actually in place were strictly limited in scope. Few furnished a living at much more than a bare subsistence level, and assistance given once might not be repeated soon again. Second, local authorities were clever about reducing the welfare price tag with strategies designed to discourage people from applying for relief. One popular tactic, used widely until the mid-twentieth century, was to list welfare recipients by name in a town's annual written report.

Private charity also existed in urban America, much of it administered via a neighborhood "settlement house." As an institution, the settlement house had its origins in mid-nineteenth century England. Settlement houses were staffed and run by trained social workers—most often women who volunteered their time, and sometimes whatever money they had as well, to the cause. These early social workers offered a wide variety of services under a single roof—kindergartens, clinics and nursing services, adult educational and recreational programs, and so on. Settlement houses did much over the years to ease conditions for immigrants trying to make new lives for themselves in America.

They did it without much help from one group of Americans who could have been an abundant source of assistance for the poor. This group was composed of the capitalists who owned the mills and mines and factories where the poor worked in good times—and where jobs might not be available in hard ones. Such was their faith in the American Dream that many leading industrialists seemed truly unaware of the need around them. Generally, those among them who did interest themselves in philanthropy were less concerned with the needs of individuals than with what they saw as the needs of society as a whole. Steel millionaire Andrew Carnegie paid for the building of public libraries around the country, while the oil-rich Rockefellers concentrated largely on medical research and educational projects. Henry Frick, also in steel, willed his New York mansion with its extensive art collection and an endowment of $15 million to the public as a museum. Such donations did much to benefit the country and enrich its culture, but they afforded little direct relief to the needy.

If capitalist philanthropy generally failed to address the reality of poverty in late nineteenth and early twentieth century America, organized religion did better. Then as now, religious groups of many faiths and creeds helped not only their own poor but the desperate of other denominations as well. The Salvation Army, active in the United States since 1880, remains one of the largest and best known of the religious charities today. Other longtime sources of assistance for the poor have been such organizations as the American Red Cross and The United Fund.

One other private charity worth special mention was New York's Children's Aid Society. This group aimed to provide foster care for homeless orphans. Between 1854 and 1929, it found homes for approximately 100,000 boys and girls. In most cases, those homes were with frontier and farming families in the West and Midwest. However well intentioned and well run this charity may have been, it can be assumed that the children it placed earned their room and board with long hours of hard work.

One reason the Children's Aid Society halted its foster care operations in 1929 was that the demand for child labor in the American West had lessened. The country was filling up; its frontier was vanishing. From now on, America would look and feel more like crowded, urbanized Europe.

From now on, its people would think more like Europeans as well, at least insofar as their ideas about public relief were concerned. Their confidence in the American Dream was about to be shaken, and the old arguments against the federal government getting involved in welfare seemed to lose relevance, for 1929 had a significance far beyond that of being the year in which the Children's Aid Society ceased its placement activities. It was also a year of economic disaster—the year the stock market crashed and the Great Depression began.

The Great Depression

The crash came in October on New York City's Wall Street, where stocks, or shares, in the nation's largest businesses and financial institutions are bought and sold. The decade of the 1920s had been a good one for the stock market. Business was booming in America and stocks were commanding higher and higher prices. Investors bought stocks, watched their value rise for a few weeks or months, and then sold at a profit. The shrewdest and luckiest investors made fortunes almost overnight. Often they had to borrow money—a great deal of money—in order to make their stock purchases; few investors had enough cash on hand to pay for all they wanted. The borrowing didn't seem to matter, though, and playing the market in the expectation that it would rise indefinitely didn't seem a risk or a gamble. It felt like betting on a sure thing.

That's why the panic that struck Wall Street on Wednesday, October 23, 1929, came as such a shock. No one knows exactly what started the panic. A rumor that some large corporation was in financial difficulty, perhaps, or the suspicion that the U.S. economy was not really as sound as it appeared. Whatever its cause, the panic upset investors, and when investors are upset, they get anxious to sell. By the time the market closed that day, a selling rampage had begun. But few wanted to buy.

The rampage and the lack of buyers continued on the twenty-fourth as stock prices plummeted. Then on Monday the twenty-eighth, the bottom fell out of the market. No one would buy. Stocks that had been worth hundreds the week before were suddenly valueless. Borrowers, and that included just about everyone on Wall Street, were asked to make good their debts. But they could not—they hadn't enough ready cash—and that meant that those from whom they had borrowed could not repay what they owed. Men who had counted themselves millionaires when the month began were suddenly penniless. Many were sunk hopelessly in debt.

The Great Depression that followed the crash was to last almost ten years and to change the life of nearly everyone who lived through it. (The depression was felt not just in the United States but throughout the industrialized world.) In the first two years after the crash, individual U.S. stock market investors lost $50 billion. Businesses were left as bankrupt as their owners. One after another, factories shut down. Thousands were thrown out of work. Between 1929 and 1932, the national income fell from $81 billion to $40 billion. Salaries and wages went from $49 billion to $29 billion, and farm income from $12 billion to less than half that.

Jobs weren't all that was lost in the Great Depression. Bank after bank failed, and since their depositors' accounts were not insured, thousands watched helplessly as their life savings vanished into thin air. The broke and jobless can't pay rent or keep up mortgage payments on a house, and even the unemployed who own their own homes may not be able to heat them or pay for needed repairs. Thousands and then more thousands of Americans were forced out onto the streets. College graduates were as desperate for jobs as the most unskilled of workers and tales were told of former millionaires selling apples on street corners.

Yet the U.S. government did nothing to help. It couldn't. Relief programs did not exist on a nationwide scale in the United States as they did in other places, and President Herbert Hoover wasn't about to ask Congress to implement such programs. Hoover was convinced that "socialistic" federal welfare programs would wreck what remained of the nation's economy.

Besides, welfare wasn't necessary, President Hoover assured the public. The United States, and indeed every industrialized country, might be going through some rough days, but left to itself, business would recover. If Americans would just be patient, things would soon bounce back to normal.

Understandably enough, millions of Americans were unimpressed with Hoover's lack of action. They saw the governments of other countries reaching out to their citizens with substantial help and thought they deserved as much from their own public institutions. Some joined socialist groups or became communists and began voicing noisy demands for social change. Others fell in line behind ultraconservative right-wingers with an ugly racist message: the nation's economic troubles were the fault of scheming Jewish businessmen or of Southern blacks who were starting to move into the large cities of the North to "steal" jobs from white Americans. The country was feeling stirrings of some of the same kind of social discontent and unrest that had pushed European leaders in the direction of national welfare a few decades earlier.

In 1932, Hoover ran for a second term of office on the Republican party ticket. The Democratic party nominee was New York Governor Franklin D. Roosevelt. Roosevelt vowed that if elected, he would offer a "new deal" to the American people—a deal that would include food for the hungry and jobs for the unemployed. Hoover made no attempt to match this promise. "Any change of policies," he cautioned, "will bring disaster to every fireside in America."

Franklin Roosevelt won the election and took the oath of office early in 1933. The changes began at once. During his first three months in the White House, Roosevelt got Congress to pass fifteen major New Deal laws. Others were enacted later at a slower pace.

The New Deal

By no means were all the new laws welfare measures. Some attempted to regulate business and banking in ways that would make future great depressions unlikely. Stock market rules were tightened up to keep investors from ever again buying stock with so much borrowed money, and a new banking law allowed the federal government to insure depositors' funds.

Other New Deal laws, though, were aimed directly at assisting the needy, in particular the unemployed. One, passed on March 31, 1933, created the Civilian Conservation Corps (CCC). Within five months, the CCC had come up with jobs for over 300,000 young men, and by the time the program was phased out fewer than ten years later, two and a half million had taken part in it. The men had planted forests, built dams to stop soil erosion, and performed other land-reclamation projects.

Another piece of early New Deal legislation established the Federal Emergency Relief Administration (FERA). Through this agency, the U.S. government directed an eventual $5 billion in federal funds to states, counties, cities, and towns, enabling them to hire thousands of workers for public construction projects. Under a third 1933 jobs program, the Public Works Administration (PWA), other public projects—bridges, dams, and housing developments—were constructed. In 1935, the PWA was replaced by the Works Projects Administration (WPA). WPA employees labored away at flood control and rural electrification, at building sewage plants and schools, and at clearing slums. In addition, WPA teachers taught classes, WPA artists decorated public buildings, WPA librarians catalogued state and municipal book collections, and WPA writers produced everything from official tourist guidebooks to successful Broadway plays.

Together, the WPA, the CCC, the PWA and the FERA represented a sort of compromise between those Americans who were demanding that the government do something to help them out and those who condemned any hint of national welfare as dangerous and unnecessary. The programs were relief programs. For the most part, though, they were relief programs of a special type—"work relief." Under them, the federal government was helping its most desperate, but not with simple handouts. Men and women were asked to put in some effort for what they got in exchange. That requirement made the programs easier for welfare opponents to swallow.

Easier—but not easy. Federal relief was still federal relief, many thought, no matter how anyone tried to dress it up in a cloak of honest labor. After all, a person who participates in a public works jobs program is not self-supporting. He or she may be getting a weekly paycheck, but since that paycheck comes from the government, the person who takes it home is just as dependent on the government as any other pauper. Work relief, in their view, boiled down to just plain relief—and they didn't like it.

Neither, in a way, did Roosevelt. It was true the president was convinced that the federal government had no choice but to step in and help out during the depression emergency. And he knew that his New Deal had succeeded in relieving suffering and giving the nation renewed hope. Even so, he was uncomfortable with the thought that his programs might prove to be the first step toward U.S. adoption of federal welfare on a broad and permanent basis. Philosophically, Roosevelt was dedicated to the principles of free enterprise and concerned about the consequences of keeping people on welfare over long periods.

The Social Security Act of 1935

In 1935, the president spoke of this concern to Congress. "Continued dependence upon relief induces a spiritual and moral disintegration, fundamentally destructive to the national fiber," he told lawmakers. "The federal government must and shall quit this business of relief." How? Through congressional willingness to approve his new Social Security bill, the president explained. The bill was designed to replace work-relief with self-help programs that would permit American workers to insure themselves against poverty.

Literally, to insure themselves. Roosevelt's bill called for the creation of a new federal agency, the Social Security Administration. This agency was to be responsible for setting up and running two social insurance programs. The first would be aimed at providing old-age pensions to retired workers; the second, unemployment benefits to the jobless. The insurance programs were to be funded through a special tax—a Social Security tax—to be levied on workers in commercial and industrial enterprises. Men and women would pay into the program throughout their working years. When they retired or lost their jobs, they could draw on the accumulated funds for assistance. That meant people would be contributing directly to covering their own future needs instead of waiting around for the government to do it for them. The argument proved persuasive with Congress, and the Social Security bill became law on August 4, 1935.

Contrary to expectations, it never did allow the U.S. government to "quit this business of relief." Instead, the Social Security Act of 1935 became the legal cornerstone of the vast array of federal social spending programs with which Americans are familiar today.

One reason things worked out that way was that although two key portions of the act had been promoted as insurance measures, they were really not quite that. An insurance program is run on the assumption that many people will pay into the program over the years but that relatively few of them will ever need to draw on it. If all goes as planned, the program's income will equal—or exceed—its outgo. Those offering the insurance will lose no money. They will make a profit. But Social Security wasn't designed to work that way. Its assumption was that everyone from whom Social Security taxes were collected was automatically entitled to receive a benefit. Furthermore, the benefits paid out to individuals may be considerably larger than the amount those individuals actually contributed in tax. That is why some rate Social Security as a form of welfare, even though most Americans do not think of it as such.

The second reason the Social Security Act of 1935 failed to get the federal government out of "this business of relief" is even simpler than the first. Far from abolishing those federal public assistance programs already in place, the law permitted them to continue—and actually added to them.

One major addition was Aid to Dependent Children (ADC), which authorized direct cash payments to children whose fathers had either died or deserted them and their mothers. The program was to be funded jointly by state and federal governments, with the federal government picking up the lion's share of the tab. The 1935 law required the federal government to help the states pay for other welfare programs as well—programs, for instance, that supplied financial aid to the aged and disabled and that offered public health care to the needy and vocational training to the jobless.

The third reason the new law did not put a halt to U.S. government relief programs was simpler still. Americans basically liked the programs. Sure, workers might grumble about Social Security taxes, but few objected when benefits began flowing in. Public medical clinics seemed less like harbingers of socialism than like a way to promote good health and make lives more productive. And how could ADC payments be said to be robbing children of their self-respect? If the Social Security Act of 1935 failed to accomplish one of its stated purposes, it was in large part because a majority of Americans wanted it that way.

What many of them wanted, as a matter of fact, was more state and federal aid, not less. And they got it. One extension of Social Security insurance benefits came as early as 1939, when the program was only four years old. In that year, Congress voted to allow funds in the system's retirement account to be used, not just to help support retired workers who had contributed to the system, but to provide for deceased workers' surviving relatives, even if those survivors had never paid any Social Security tax at all. In 1957, the program was broadened again, this time to permit payments to workers injured or disabled on the job. Social Security benefit levels have been raised, as well, and its coverage expanded to include household and farm workers, members of the Armed Forces and the clergy, most state and local government employees, and many of the self-employed. The ADC section of the original Social Security Act was also liberalized. In 1950, the program was renamed Aid to Families with Dependent Children—AFDC—and the mothers of dependent children added to its rolls. In some states, even fathers may benefit.

There is a fourth reason the federal government found itself as a permanent provider of relief, found itself indeed enlarging upon that role year by year. This reason is the simplest of all: the need did not go away. No matter how much the United States poured into its welfare programs—millions of dollars at first, then billions—more always seemed to be required.

It was that way from the start. Not even the jobs programs of the early New Deal, programs that seemed so bold at the time, were enough to erase poverty in the United States, and neither was Social Security. Unemployment and retirement insurance, ADC, WPA, and the rest helped Americans to cope with the depression, but they did not put an end to it. Only in the 1940s, when the United States became involved in World War II and American mines, mills, and factories geared up for war production, did the economy really prosper. The prosperity continued after the war ended in 1945 and right through most of the 1950s. These were the years during which America's well-to-do suburbs mushroomed, its building industry flourished, and its shoppers launched a buying spree in the bright new malls that were beginning to dot the landscape. They were years when most people took it for granted that they would be richer, better-educated and happier than their parents had been—and that their children would be better off still. Almost hidden by the general prosperity, though, a desperate new poverty was materializing.

The Other America

It was a poverty unlike that of the depression years, when want and need had been spread out more or less evenly across the land. The new poverty was limited to isolated pockets. Many of these pockets could be found in the rural South. Poverty was evident in run-down West Virginia coal-mining towns, for example, where work was dirty, dangerous, and ill-paid—when it was available at all. Poverty lurked along the back roads of states like Alabama, Georgia, and Mississippi, where the black descendants of America's slaves lived in tar-paper shacks and got starvation wages in return for long days of drudgery in white men's fields and homes. It was sprinkled generously across the rugged Appalachian foothills whose exhausted soil could no longer support all who tried to live upon it.

Pockets of poverty existed in the great cities of the Northeast and Midwest, too. There they were often the result of southerners moving north in search of manufacturing and factory work. Although many of the migrants landed jobs, others did not, either because the jobs were not there or they lacked the skills to fill them. Blacks—and a hefty percentage of the new arrivals were black—discovered that the racial prejudice against them was as strong in the North as it had been in the South. They faced discrimination in the workplace and in housing, education, and the use of public facilities such as restaurants and restrooms.

Still other poverty pockets could be seen in the farming states of the West and Midwest. There, small family farms were giving way to "agribusiness," agriculture as big business. Companies that owned thousands upon thousands of acres—and that also owned sophisticated machinery capable of plowing, planting, cultivating, and harvesting that land quickly and cheaply—could easily outproduce and undersell the hardest-working of individual farmers with their limited acreage and old-fashioned tools and methods. Many, forced from their farms, joined other displaced Americans in an increasingly difficult hunt for jobs.

But until the early 1960s, the majority of white, suburban, middle-class Americans knew little of the nation's poverty pockets. It took a book—a slim volume written by a young social activist named Michael Harrington—to jolt the country and alert it to the reality of want in the midst of plenty.

Harrington's book, published in 1962, was aptly titled *The Other America*. It told, in simple but vivid human terms, of the author's travels throughout Appalachia and the Northeast and across the country's depressed farm belt. It described the hopeless men and despairing women of the rural South and the northern ghetto. It described their children, too—children who were, thanks to poor nutrition and primitive sanitary conditions, all too often growing up mentally or physically stunted, or not living to grow up at all. "It is an

45

outrage and a scandal that there should be such social misery," Harrington wrote.

Hundreds of thousands of appalled Americans agreed. One of them was the country's president, John F. Kennedy. Determined to put an end to the kind of want portrayed in *The Other America*, the president urged Congress to enact legislation aimed at eliminating poverty in the United States once and for all. One result of that determination was the food stamp program, which allowed the federal government to subsidize food purchases for individuals whose income falls below a so-called "poverty line." (In 1965, that line was set at $3,223 for a nonfarm family of four; in 1987, reflecting two decades of inflation, it was $11,611 for the same size family.) The federal Department of Agriculture was to allot food stamps to qualified families and individuals on the basis of their incomes. The stamps, available in $1, $5, and $10 denominations, might be exchanged for food items.

But the food stamp program was only one piece of legislation, and before Kennedy could get others, he was dead. On November 22, 1963, the president was shot by an assassin in Dallas, Texas. The responsibility for leading the fight against poverty fell to his vice-president and successor, Lyndon B. Johnson.

The War on Poverty

The new president pledged to work with Congress in an all-out "war on poverty." The war would end in victory, Johnson promised, in the creation of what he called the Great Society.

For a while, it looked as if that promise would be kept. Much of the middle-class public backed the president's antipoverty program wholeheartedly. Public enthusiasm was mirrored in Congress, which began passing Great Society legislation at once.

The laws Congress enacted in 1964 and 1965 were designed to attack poverty on three major fronts. First were those aimed at providing new or expanded programs of direct relief. The second group of laws established a number of job and job-training programs. The third, and most controversial, part of the Great Society program was an attempt to end poverty by eliminating what Johnson and his aides saw as some of its root causes—racism and political powerlessness among certain groups of Americans.

Programs of direct relief constituted that portion of the War on Poverty that was the easiest to implement. At Johnson's urging, Congress raised AFDC payments and enabled more families to participate in the program. Social Security unemployment benefits were upped. New programs included Medicare, enacted in 1965 to offer federal medical insurance to men and women age sixty-five or over as well as to the disabled on Social Security. Those enrolled in the program pay for it through a monthly premium, which is added onto a worker's Social Security tax. Medicaid, also established in 1965, benefits persons of all ages on welfare. Unlike Medicare, Medicaid is administered on a state-by-state basis, and its costs are borne jointly by state and federal governments.

The second prong of the Johnson War on Poverty involved jobs and job training and education. The Job Corps, established and funded under the Economic Opportunity Act of 1964, aimed at preparing young people—in particular, young people from the nation's poverty pockets—"for the responsibility of citizenship" and to "increase their employability." Job Corps employment was offered through each state individually, rather than through the federal government. Federal job-training funds were also made available to the states by means of the Manpower Development and Training Act. The Vocational Education Act sent federal monies to the states to establish vocational training centers, and the Higher Education Facilities Act gave grants to colleges and universities and allowed federal tax dollars to be used for low-cost student loans. Under the Head Start program, the federal government enabled towns and cities to provide pre-kindergarten schooling for disadvantaged boys and girls. Head Start was subsequently expanded to include children at all income levels. Families that can afford to pay for its programs do so on a sliding scale.

The third part of the War on Poverty—the assault on racism and political powerlessness—reflected the president's conviction that poverty owes its existence at least as much to social, political, and economic conditions as to individual deficiencies or bad character. Johnson was a self-made man in what he liked to think of as the best American tradition. He washed cars and dishes, ran an elevator and picked fruit before becoming a teacher, rancher, politician, and television station owner. But the fact that Johnson prided himself on having worked his own way up to the top did not blind him to the knowledge that, as a white man, he had been in a better position to do so than if he had been black or a member of some other minority. That knowledge prompted him to assume a special mission to wipe out inequalities based on race and ethnic origin.

And so he asked Congress to approve a civil rights bill banning racial discrimination in jobs, housing, and the use of public accommodations. Congress passed the legislation on June 29, 1964. A little over a year later, on August 6, 1965, Johnson signed a second historic measure, the Voting Rights Act. It permitted federal authorities to intervene in places where state and local laws and customs had allowed white officials to keep black citizens from taking part in elections. The president hoped that the new laws would bring minorities into the political process and into the job market, thereby giving them a better chance to move out of the ghetto—and out of poverty. If the laws accomplished that, he thought, blacks and others who faced discrimination would at last have a fair shot at the American Dream.

But things didn't work out quite that way.

4

The Welfare "Mess"—
One Point of View

The programs of Lyndon Johnson's War on Poverty never did produce the Great Society that the president had envisioned. Still, a number of them contributed to making life better for millions of Americans. The Voting Rights Act brought blacks and Hispanics first to the polls and then into government. Many of the unemployed who took advantage of job-training programs learned to apply their newly acquired skills toward earning a decent wage. Head Start children tended to be more successful in their early school years than did children who had not participated in the program. Food stamps and public health benefits meant healthier and longer lives for young and old alike. Increased AFDC payments enabled many a poor family to raise its standards of living.

But by no means did the laws accomplish all they were intended to. Racial discrimination was too deeply embedded in American society and in American attitudes to disappear overnight. To this day, blacks and other minority group members continue to be under-represented in schools, colleges, business, the professions, and government. Nor was poverty to be so easily vanquished, and to the disappointment of many, the War on Poverty seemed to be in trouble from the start. There were those who accused Johnson himself of being to blame for that.

The War on Poverty—Why Did it Fail?

Johnson doomed the War on Poverty, these people said, when he insisted on involving the country in another war, the war in Vietnam. Hostilities in that Southeast Asian land had already been going on for years when Johnson entered the White House. The fighting was between the anticommunist government of South Vietnam on one side and South Vietnamese rebels, helped by the forces of communist North Vietnam, on the other. The rebels' goal, and that of the communist north, was to unify the divided country under one single government. Such a government would almost certainly be communist—a prospect Johnson and other presidents found troubling. The U.S. government, therefore, assisted South Vietnam's anticommunist rulers with money, weapons, and military advice.

Even so, South Vietnam seemed to be losing, and in 1964, Johnson made up his mind to join in the actual fighting. Within months, the United States was deeply engaged on the battlefield. In all, just under nine million Americans were to serve in the war. Nearly 60,000 died. Besides being expensive in human terms, the war cost a great deal of money. At the height of U.S. involvement in 1967, this country was spending $57.6 million a day—$40,000 a minute—to pay for it.

Money going to Vietnam meant money not going to the War on Poverty. Funding for the whole jobs and job-training portion of Johnson's antipoverty effort amounted to $800 million in 1964—$1522 a minute. A sizeable sum, but only a tiny fraction, critics like Michael Harrington pointed out, of what was being spent in Vietnam. Overall, federal jobs programs got just $6 billion between 1964 and 1968, not nearly enough, Harrington maintained twenty years later, to have provided the employment and produced the skills that might have allowed the bulk of the nation's poor to work their way out of poverty.

Was that why the War on Poverty failed? Had the effort fallen victim to a lack of funds? Liberals and social activists like Michael Harrington might think so, but in fact that was nonsense, other Americans said. These Americans, most of whom shared conservative social, political, and economic ideas, believed the War on Poverty failed because of its own built-in flaws.

Yes, conservatives conceded, huge amounts of money had gone to Southeast Asia between 1964 and 1973. But huge amounts also went to battling poverty and providing relief for the needy. Federal welfare spending rose every year of the Johnson administration. It went up while his successor, conservative Republican Richard M. Nixon (president from 1969 to 1974), was in office too. It continued to increase under another Republican president, Gerald R. Ford (1974-1977) and from 1977 to 1981 under Democrat Jimmy Carter. No one could rightly say that the War on Poverty and its social welfare programs were not adequately funded, the conservatives contended.

In fact, they added, the funding was more than adequate; it was exorbitantly high. "A monstrous, consuming outrage," President Nixon labeled the spending, and the welfare system itself, in 1971. The year before, AFDC expenditures had amounted to $4.1 billion. Compare that to an AFDC bill of $621 million in 1955. Aid to the blind cost $8,446,000 in 1970; aid to the disabled, $91,325,000, and so on. According to financial writer Henry Hazlitt, the nation's total spending for all social welfare programs, including Social Security insurance, came to a whopping $171 billion by the early seventies.

And the irony was, conservatives went on, that all the spending had not eliminated need or solved the nation's welfare problem. America's relief population actually increased during the War on Poverty years.

"The rise in the welfare rolls was from 7 million in 1962 to 16 million in 1972," William F. Buckley, Jr., wrote in his 1973 book *Four Reforms: A Program for the 70s*. Buckley, a columnist and television commentator on American public affairs, is, like Hazlitt, a conservative and an outspoken critic of past and present U.S. welfare policies. In *Four Reforms* he defended his position with facts and figures.

According to Buckley, 10 percent of the black residents of New York City were on public assistance in 1961. By 1971, the percentage had risen to 35. Between 1960 and 1970, California relief recipients went from 600,000 to almost two and a quarter million. At that point, their numbers were growing by 40,000 a month. Buckley neglected to point out, however, that much of that growth could be explained by the large number of people moving to California during those years.

Figures from other sources supported Buckley's. Hazlitt presented a slew of them in his book *The Conquest of Poverty,* which also appeared in 1973. New Yorkers of all races on relief rose from 328,000 in 1960 to 1,275,000 in August 1972, Hazlitt wrote—a total that exceeded the entire population of Baltimore, Maryland. In 1971, the federal government's Department of Health, Education, and Welfare (reorganized in 1979 as the Department of Health and Human Services—HHS) reported that more than 10 percent of the residents of the country's twenty largest cities received public assistance payments that year.

To conservatives, then, as to liberals, the War on Poverty had to be reckoned a disappointment. Not only had it failed to eliminate want and need, but it had done so at a time when—as conservatives saw it—poverty and welfare should have been shrinking problems, not growing ones, because the 1960s were a time of economic prosperity in the United States. Employment rose during the decade and so did salaries. In 1960, 65.7 million Americans had jobs. Five years later, 71 million were employed, and five years after that, 78.6 million. Over the same period, the average weekly salary for someone with a job in manufacturing went from $89.72 to $107.53 to $133.33.

How did the statistics translate into real life? Buckley had an answer. Starting with the poverty-line estimates worked out by the Johnson administration—that a nonfarm family of four was "poor" if its income fell below $3,223 in 1965, for example—and adjusting those estimates for inflation and other economic changes, Buckley concluded that fully half the country had been poor in 1920. Forty years later, by his reckoning, the figure had been cut to 20 percent. It dropped to 11 percent in 1967 and to less than 9 percent at the time he was working on *Four Reforms*. Would the decline Buckley saw in poverty continue in the 1970s and 1980s? Henry Hazlitt, for one, though it would—providing capitalism and free enterprise were given the opportunity to grow and to create new jobs. If they did get that opportunity, there would be fewer demands on the welfare system. "In the United States," Hazlitt wrote "the problem of relief . . . is . . . likely to be of constantly diminishing importance . . . "

Hazlitt's optimism was badly misplaced, as he would doubtless be among the first to admit. In the years following his book's publication, the country's relief problems worsened. The number of Americans on welfare went right on growing throughout the 1970s as it had in the sixties. AFDC recipients, for example, who had numbered about 9.5 million at the beginning of the decade, had increased to over 11 million by its end. Federal, state and local welfare costs soared along with case loads. And the increases had taken place against a backdrop that still included signs of economic strength. Salaries and employment levels continued their rise in the 1970s, for instance. In 1980, 99 million Americans held jobs, and in the next year the number of employed topped 100 million. Factory workers who had earned $133.33 a week in 1970 were getting $190.79 five years later. In 1980, they were bringing home a weekly $288.63.

So what was wrong? Why wasn't poverty disappearing and, with it, the need for programs of public assistance as Hazlitt had predicted? How could record prosperity be combined with record relief costs? Why should a country with a growing economy also have a growing welfare burden?

Why shouldn't it, many Americans would retort, given the fact that U.S. relief systems and programs are such a mess? From the outset, those systems and programs were based on the idea that government can and should try to eradicate poverty with handouts of cash and other benefits. The premise was faulty to begin with, the critics said, and to make things worse, nearly all the programs grounded in it were poorly thought out, badly designed, and carelessly run. They never stood a chance of eliminating either poverty or the demand for welfare. What they did was to lead to increases in both and create more problems than they solved.

What problems in particular? The one most critics would probably mention first can be summed up in a word: cheating. The idea that American taxpayers are the hapless victims of widespread welfare fraud is an article of faith among much of the nonrelief population.

"Cheats" and "Chiselers"

Certainly Americans read enough about welfare cheats in the daily paper and hear enough about them on radio and television. "Welfare Loophole Forces City to Pay Up," cries a typical smalltown newspaper headline. According to the article, a local welfare couple spent $50 of the money it received in local general assistance funds on Christmas presents for themselves and their children. Now, penniless and facing the coming winter with an empty fuel tank, the family had applied for a new relief grant. Given the choice between honoring the request and sending children home to a cold apartment, city officials elected to make the grant.

Americans don't have to search the news media to find examples of what they may consider to be the misuse of welfare funds. Many believe they see such incidents every day. Take the use of food stamps. What shopper hasn't watched someone spend allotted stamps on candy bars, cookies, soda, or potato chips?

Store checkout clerks have their own food stamp tales to tell. "It really bothers me," says a woman named Sandy who works part time in the mom and pop grocery that serves her small farming community. "Most of them don't cheat, but the ones that do get me so mad. They come in here with their stamps and use them for some little thing—a pack of gum. Then they take their change and buy beer."

Actually, food stamp rules are designed to discourage that sort of behavior, and anyone who owns or works in a store authorized to accept food stamps is required to know the rules and abide by them.

Clerks are supposed to make sure that the stamps go for food items and nothing else—no paper goods, cosmetics, health aids, or cleaning products, for example. They may not hand out more than 99 cents worth of change at a time. A shopper who pays for a 99-cent purchase with a $10 stamp must accept nine $1 stamps and 1 cent in change. By law, $5 stamps and $10 stamps are never given in change. Store owners who break the rules, or who permit their clerks to do so, can be fined or kept from accepting food stamps in the future.

But food stamp recipients have their ways of getting around the regulations, Sandy complains. "They come in over and over, and buy this or that. By night, they've got enough cash for a six-pack."

Sandy is especially irritated by the nagging feeling that unscrupulous food stamp customers take pleasure in getting away with their petty frauds. "They buy something for $4.99," she explains, "and they know they're only going to get a penny change. So they pick up a couple pieces of penny candy. That means they'll be paying $5.01 and getting 99 cents back. Betty [Sandy's boss] says when that happens, give them the candy for free and don't let them have the money. So you do. But then they pick up another piece of candy. And you say, 'OK, take that, too.' Then they pick up another piece and another, until you have to give in and let them have the change."

Disheartening as it is for honest citizens to hear anecdotes of this kind, the nickel and dime misuse of food stamps amounts to no more than the tip of the welfare fraud iceberg. Or so some claim, although most welfare professionals would disagree. Of all the supposed frauds around, the ones that seem to be mentioned most frequently, and with the greatest amount of resentment, are those perpetrated by the women served by the Aid to Families with Dependent Children program.

Aid to Families with Dependent Children

AFDC was, as we know, originally called Aid to Dependent Children and began as part of President Franklin Roosevelt's New Deal. At that time, only the children of fathers not living at home, who had either died or deserted their families, were eligible to receive payments. After 1950, the mothers of absent-father children became eligible as well.

Another rules change came about because of criticism of the program as antifamily. By refusing benefits to families in which the husband and father was present, the critics said, AFDC officials practically forced indigent men to desert their wives and children. So federal law was changed to allow each state to decide for itself whether or not to make AFDC aid available to families in which the father was present but unemployed, handicapped, or unable for some other reason to support his offspring. About half the states did agree to permit AFDC-Unemployed Parent (AFDC-UP) payments.

To begin to understand why AFDC rouses so much popular antagonism, it's important to note that it differs from other types of social welfare such as job training or Medicare. Medicare is an insurance program. Those enrolled in it also contribute to it by paying a monthly premium. A job-training program requires beneficiaries to put forth some effort to work and learn. But AFDC is what Americans think of as a handout and nothing else. Those who take from the program are not asked to give anything back in return. To many Americans, that makes it seem as if AFDC recipients do not earn or deserve the help they get.

How much help? In 1987, the average person on AFDC in Massachusetts was getting $182.70 a month. Elsewhere, people were getting less; in Alabama, the 1987 personal average was $39.29 monthly. Why the variation? One reason is state-to-state differences in living costs. Plainly, it costs less to live in Chickasaw, Alabama, than in Boston, Massachusetts. The state with the lowest level of payments in 1987 was Mississippi—$38.54 per person per month—and the one with the highest was Alaska—$228.45. Average for the nation was $122.93. Added up, the AFDC bill came to $16,322,557,650 in 1987.

Small wonder taxpayers questioned the program. Their questions became more insistent every time they heard charges of fraud within the program—a charge they heard frequently. An especially authoritative sounding one came in 1987 from Richard P. Kusserow, inspector general of the federal Department of Health and Human Services. According to him, AFDC officials had paid out a full *$1 billion* in false claims the previous year. Kusserow's study, which took a critical look at AFDC rules and procedures, suggested that as much as $800 million could be saved each year if all applicants were more carefully screened before officials began payments. Screening would have made it harder for a woman like Donna Gilbeau, whom we met in Chapter 1, to have robbed the U.S. government and the state of Maine of $70,000 between 1977 and 1984, for instance. Taking a closer look at applicants might also make it more difficult for families in which an ablebodied and employed father only pretends to be absent, while actually remaining at home, to get away with their frauds.

Why weren't AFDC administrators more careful about examining AFDC applications? For one thing, the program had no "provision . . . providing for . . . sanctions against perpetrators of fraud," Kusserow's report pointed out. Unlike the food stamp program, AFDC had no systematic safeguards in place to guard against rule-breaking. Besides, Kusserow went on, the states had no strong financial motive for rooting out fraud. Since the federal government had always borne so much of the AFDC burden—up to 80 percent of the total bill in some cases—each individual state's fraud losses were relatively small. He recommended that Congress set up a federal antifraud unit to work with the states "to more sharply focus management attention on the prevention, deterrence and detection of fraud."

Would such a unit be able to solve the fraud problem? Perhaps, although plenty of Americans had their doubts about that, and about some of the fraud charges leveled against AFDC mothers and other so-called welfare cheats, as well. We will see other, and very different, points of view on the subject of welfare fraud in the next chapter. We'll also take a closer look at Kusserow's rather unusual definition of the word "fraud" itself. But even if the country did save $800 million a year—or even a billion—that would not be enough to stop the complaints about AFDC. The reason: the kind of welfare cheating addressed in the HHS report was not the kind that seemed to bother AFDC critics most. What really roused their ire was their conviction that there are thousands of women all across the country giving birth for no other reason than to make themselves eligible for benefits.

Such women are common—of that, the critics had no doubt. It's possible that the vehemence of Sandy's feelings about small-time thievery among her food stamp customers flows in part from her assumption that a lot of them cheated in a more serious fashion every time they had a baby. Sandy claims to have seen hints of such cheating even among her own former in-laws. At one point, she contends, her ex-husband's sister, already the sixteen-year-old mother of one, seriously considered becoming pregnant again just to raise her benefit level.

Whether or not unscrupulous women were "getting themselves" pregnant to qualify for welfare was a debatable point, but the charge was nothing new in late twentieth-century America. What were people saying about that in England a couple hundred years ago? "To the woman, a single illegitimate child is seldom any expense, and two or three are a source of positive profit." According to Hazlitt, this statement "could easily pass as a description of such conditions in, say, New York City in 1972."

Conservatives were not the only ones voicing complaints about the number of AFDC children society is forced to support. In a 1988 column in *The New York Times*, the city's Democratic mayor, Edward Koch, directed public attention to a family consisting of a father with four girlfriends and nineteen children. All twenty-four were residing at government expense in welfare hotels around the city. "Is it really government's responsibility to provide [this man], the mothers of his children and those nineteen children with shelter?" Koch demanded.

The mayor expressed a displeasure that went beyond the sheer number of AFDC recipients. Something was badly askew with welfare lifestyles and opportunities, as well, he protested. Koch described one welfare mother whom he visited at her home in the Bronx. The mother and her three children were living in "a tastefully furnished apartment," Koch noted, one renovated by the city at a cost of $65,000. "When I walked in," he went on, "the children were sitting on the couch watching a very large television set with the volume turned up loud. On top of the set was a VCR." A VCR? A "very large television" with the "volume turned up loud"? But it wasn't so much the luxury of the family's surroundings that shocked—his own word—the mayor. It was the fact that the mother had turned down nineteen different apartments offered her by city officials before moving into this one. Koch listened in disbelief as she explained her pickiness. "Either [the rejected apartments] weren't located in nice buildings or nice neighborhoods, or they weren't [where] I wanted to live."

"Something has gone wrong," Koch told his readers. "I thought to myself, people who are part of the working poor, and who are perhaps either doubled up or living in substandard housing, would be furious if they knew they'd been denied the opportunity to take one of those nineteen apartments this woman had turned down." People on welfare are spoiled, that was what the column implied.

A great many who read it probably shared the sentiment. It's a popular belief that people on relief enjoy a higher standard of living than do the working poor. So generous had U.S. benefits become by the late 1980s that even non-cheaters shrewd enough to apply for all of those available, AFDC, food stamps, housing and fuel allowances, scholarship, job training, medical care, Head Start, work-study programs, auto insurance, travel subsidies, and so on, could live better than anyone working for the minimum wage—that was the common view.

That no one could live well on the minimum wage was undeniably true. Under federal law, that minimum was $3.35 an hour for nonfarm workers in 1988, although some states had their own higher levels. What incentive does $3.35 an hour give a welfare recipient to take

59

minimum-wage work if it is offered? At that rate, a person could work an eight-hour day, five days a week, fifty-two weeks of the year, and end up with $6,968. Naturally, people would rather be on relief than on their own. That was another thing wrong with AFDC, the program's critics said: it encouraged dependency.

Welfare Dependency

All welfare programs had been designed and set up in ways that encourage dependency—that was the second major flaw many Americans saw in them. The idea that the lazy and shiftless cannot resist going—and staying—on welfare is nothing new, of course. The nineteenth-century English workhouse system grew directly out of it. But is the idea correct?

Critics like Hazlitt and Buckley would say so. Not even the emergency of the Great Depression of the 1930s was enough to justify the kind of "welfarism" introduced into the country by Roosevelt's New Deal. Americans would have done better to have listened to candidate Hoover during the 1932 election campaign and trusted to their own hard work and effort to pull them out of the economic morass. But they didn't. They chose welfare—dependency—over old-fashioned capitalism—freedom. Since then, the country has been paying, literally paying, for their choice.

And the War on Poverty only made matters worse, conservative thinkers go on. It turned welfare into a "growth industry" in the United States. How? The Economic Opportunity Act of 1964, the heart of Johnson's antipoverty program, included a provision that actually required the federal government itself to seek out those who might qualify for welfare and bring them into the system.

Required government to try to get more people onto relief? Yes, Hazlitt wrote in *The Conquest of Poverty*. The law authorized the hiring of 100,000 men and women to staff Community Action Agencies around the country. "One of the major tasks of this legion was to tell poor people about welfare," Hazlitt quotes the conservative sociologist Nathan Glazer as saying. To go beyond merely telling them about it, too, Glazer continued. The agencies' mandate was to "accompany [welfare applicants] to welfare agencies, argue for them, organize them . . . distribute simplified accounts of the rules governing welfare and the benefits available."

So that's why the nation's welfare rolls are increasing! The activities of Community Action Agencies also help to explain why 40,000 new men, women, and children in California were going on relief every month by 1971, the critics said, and why the welfare population of New York City had outstripped the entire citizenry of Baltimore. Congress had established a cadre of welfare professionals dedicated to recruiting applicants for relief, inciting them to militancy in their demands for more and more aid, and rendering them dependent upon the system. At least that was how Glazer and others saw matters.

What was more, the Community Action Agencies were only part of the recruitment story, Glazer went on. In addition, "there were at least 1,800 lawyers" working through the Office of Economic Opportunity. "One of their functions," in Glazer's words, "was to challenge the restrictions around the granting of welfare." That meant taking cities and states to court in an endeavor to overturn rules and regulations that limited the people's eligibility for welfare. Examples of such laws might be ones that denied benefits to mothers capable of working or that kept children from getting AFDC payments if their fathers' whereabouts were known. What the War on Poverty came to then, as far as its conservative critics could tell, was a plan to give Americans lessons in the fine art of tapping the public purse.

And lessons in welfare militancy. In 1966, a riot started in Cleveland after police allegedly mistreated a relief recipient who had been attempting to collect public money to pay for a decent funeral for a fellow recipient who had just died. The next year in Boston, egged on by militant social advocates, welfare clients staged a protest sit-in at a welfare office. They were beaten by police, and three days of rioting followed. The War on Poverty seemed to have become a war indeed. That constituted yet another problem in conservative eyes. The country had undertaken to wage an all-out offensive against want and need, and how had the poor reacted? With ingratitude at best and with violence at worst.

Welfare Organization

Another problem many saw in U.S. welfare concerned organization. Individual programs were as deeply flawed and as unworkable as is the overall system, they thought. We've already seen how critics like HHS's Richard Kusserow believe that AFDC fraud problems were worsened by poorly written rules and lax enforcement policies. Design deficiencies in other programs presented problems as well.

Take Social Security. It isn't a relief program, but it *is* part of the country's social welfare system. And it's about as straightforward and financially valid as one of those chain letters that asks you to send five dollars to the name at the top of the list and put your own name at the bottom. The scheme's promise is that you, in your turn, will get hundreds—maybe thousands—in cash from those whose names go on the list below yours. It doesn't usually work out that way though and generally only the first few people in the chain make any money. The rest follow the directions faithfully but receive nothing back. It's much the same for every American working and paying the Social Security tax today, says Nobel Prize-winning economist Milton Friedman. Projections for future solvency of the program vary, and no one can be sure that when his or her turn to collect retirement and survivorship benefits comes around, the money will be there.

Friedman made his comparison between Social Security and chain letters (which are illegal, by the way, if they use the mails to ask for money) in *Free to Choose*, a book he coauthored with his wife, Rose. Like any other pyramid scheme, the Friedmans wrote, "Social Security . . . has been promoted . . . through misleading labelling and deceptive advertising." How so? "The impression is given that a worker's 'benefits' are financed by his 'contributions.'" They are not, the authors contend. Instead, the tax each worker pays into the Social

Security system goes to support the retirees and survivors of an earlier generation. Present-day workers aren't saving up to pay for their own old age—they're too busy paying the bills for their parents and grandparents. They'll have to trust their children and grandchildren to foot the bill for them thirty or forty years from now. But will the younger generation be willing to assume that burden? The Friedmans do not think so.

Their pessimism about the system is founded on more than the suspicion that future generations may balk at supporting their elders. Another trouble is that America's elderly and retired population is growing so fast, much faster than the population of younger workers. In 1950, the Friedmans say, seventeen men and women were working—and paying Social Security tax—for each retiree or survivor drawing out from the system. Twenty years later, only three were working for each one being supported, and by early in the next century, they warn, the ratio may fall to two workers for every beneficiary. It doesn't take a mathematical genius to realize that if two people are supporting a third, each one is going to have to pay out a great deal more than if seventeen are sharing the job. According to Gary Allen, editor of the extremely conservative *American Opinion* magazine, the maximum yearly Social Security tax a worker had to pay in 1960 was $144. In 1970, it was $405, and in 1980, $1588. Inflation has contributed to the rise, of course, but so have the costs of increased benefits. If Social Security taxes continue to go up, Allen warned, taxpayers will rebel and refuse to pay them. Eventually the system will become bankrupt.

The whole country will end in bankruptcy if something isn't done, and done soon, not just about Social Security, but about the whole welfare mess, the conservative critics were prophesying. One reason: Americans had gotten into the habit of allowing the poor themselves to decide whether or not they were poor.

What is poor? Or rather, what is poverty like in the United States?

Some say we can start to answer that question only by asking another: What is poverty like outside the United States? In the Latin

American nation of Haiti, the average per-person income was $300 in the mid-1980s. Unemployment stood at 50 percent of the adult population in 1988. Halfway around the world in Bangladesh, the average income was $113 a year. In the United States, a single man or woman can have an income totaling $5,469—forty-eight times that of the average citizen of Bangladesh—and still be officially "poor."

Of course, it costs more to live in the United States than it does in Bangladesh. But that's because the standard of living is so much higher here. To be "poor" in America is to be fabulously wealthy or, at the very least, comfortably well off in a country like Bangladesh or Haiti. Poverty in the United States just isn't like poverty elsewhere in the world. In many countries, the poor sleep in the streets and eat a handful of rice each day, or they eat nothing at all. If they want fresh uncontaminated water, they may have to buy it. An American may be "poor" and yet own a house and a car—or cars—a VCR, and television and other luxuries. He or she may eat three square meals a day.

So what is "poor" really in America? In January 1964, President Johnson's Council of Economic Advisors defined it, in part, as "the inability to satisfy minimum demands." To have a decent standard of living, that is. But what's decent or minimal? A handful of rice? Meat loaf and a baked potato? "Each of us might have his own conception of a 'decent' standard," Hazlitt wrote, "and every family might have its own ideas of its 'needs.'" For one family, rice may seem enough. For another, meat loaf is the minimum. Let society provide the former, and they will demand the latter. Give them that, and they'll want to move up to steak. Any system of public relief that permits recipients to live at a point above the bare subsistence level—as American relief does—or that allows them to improve their standard of living at its expense—as American relief does—"will in the end do more harm than good to the whole community," conservative critics conclude.

By the time the 1970s ended, a good many Americans had evidently come to share that perspective. Or, if they didn't exactly share it, they were at least willing to look the other way when their leaders acted upon it. In 1980, Ronald W. Reagan was elected president of the United States. He came to the White House promising to cut relief spending.

A Promise of Change

A very conservative Republican, Reagan was, like Buckley or Hazlitt, possessed by the idea of the American Dream. Welfare and the dependency it caused were undermining that dream, he thought. Only if Congress would help him cut antipoverty spending would it survive. Once the poor learned they would no longer be getting free government handouts, they would buckle down to the kind of hard work that success demands. Then at last, poverty would be defeated.

Other politicians had tried to reduce social welfare spending. Few had been able to do so. Would Reagan?

In some ways, it seemed unlikely. Many of our programs of social welfare are so-called entitlement programs. In passing the laws that established these programs, Congress said that Americans are "entitled" to share in their benefits. Once an entitlement program is in place, it is nearly impossible to cut back on it.

When it came to nonentitlement programs, however, Reagan could anticipate greater success. Spending for such programs is known as "discretionary," and it is up to lawmakers to use their own judgment as to whether or not to continue it. Discretionary spending can be reduced by a determined president and a willing Congress. Reagan made no secret of his determination.

And Congress seemed as if it might be willing to go along. Why? As the 1980s began, the U.S. economy was in trouble. Inflation had struck in the seventies, and the federal Department of Labor estimated that the cost of living was rising at the rate of almost 14 percent a year. Salaries were going up as well, but not enough. The factory worker who had been taking home $133.33 in 1970 was getting more than twice that—$288.62—in 1980. In terms of buying power, however, the increase amounted to a measly $4 a week.

To make things worse, the menace of unemployment hung over

the nation's work force. In 1970, the jobless rate had stood at under 5 percent. Ten years later, it was over 7 percent—and climbing. The absolute number of those employed was about to fall too, from 100 million employed Americans in 1981 to about 99.5 million in 1982. The dip in employment figures came despite a growing population.

Most ominous of all, in the opinion of economists and financial experts, was the fact that the country was badly in debt. In 1970, the national debt had come to about $370 billion. In 1980, it was $998 billion.

The national debt scared people. But, at the same time, it seemed somehow remote from their lives. Joblessness and inflation, which hit closer to home, scared them even more. No longer did mainstream middle-class Americans have the absolute confidence in their own future that they had enjoyed in earlier years. No longer could they feel certain that tomorrow would always be better than today or that greater prosperity lay right around the corner. Rather, people worried about losing what they already had.

People who know that they are economically insecure in this way are unlikely to have much sympathy for those who look to them for support, as relief recipients do. They are more apt to resent those who ask them for their hard-earned tax dollars. Congress, well aware of that resentment, seemed inclined to support Reagan's budget-cutting plans.

Their support was strengthened by presidential assurances on how the budget-cutting would be carried out. Programs and services that tended to encourage laziness or welfare dependency would be tightened up or eliminated. But for the truly needy, little would change. A "safety net" of programs would remain in place for them. Some in Congress and around the country questioned whether "holes" in that net would allow some of the poor to slip through, but Reagan said not. Anyway, private charities could always step in and help out in an emergency. Such was their traditional role.

That argument and the safety net idea apparently clinched the argument. Congressional minds were at ease as Ronald Reagan stepped up to take the oath of office.

5

The Mess Revisited—
Other Views

Ronald Reagan became the fortieth president of the United States on Tuesday, January 20, 1981. At that point, discretionary domestic spending amounted to 5.7 percent of the gross national product (GNP). The GNP is the monetary value of all the nation's goods and services produced during a specified period, usually a year.

The promised budget-cutting began almost immediately. It continued throughout the four years of Reagan's first term of office and well into his second.

Federal spending for education and job training dropped from $33 billion to $28 billion. Community development programs, programs of neighborhood improvement, went down by $4.5 billion, from $10.5 billion to $6 billion. Food stamp funding was reduced by 18.8 percent and other nutrition programs by 13.3 percent. A million low-income children were removed from nutrition programs between 1982 and 1984. (In 1984, nutrition spending was restored to earlier levels.) AFDC slipped 17.7 percent, and 600,000 people were excluded from Medicaid.

Even more drastic were cuts in federal housing assistance. According to the public interest group Common Cause, "the number of households slated for new housing aid fell to about 74,000 [in 1987] compared to 192,000 new units in ... 1980 and a peak of 393,000 new units three years before that." The federal agency responsible for supervising public housing construction, the Department of Housing and Urban Development (HUD), saw its total departmental budget slashed by well over 50 percent. Overall, federal discretionary domestic spending was lowered to just 3.7 percent of the GNP. That meant that over five years, Congress and the administration had cooperated in reducing such spending by an astonishing 35 percent.

In practical terms, the cut was even greater than that. Why? Inflation. Prices rose 32 percent between 1981 and 1988. That meant an effective cut of 32 percent even for programs in which funding levels remained constant. Where levels were reduced, those reductions had to be tacked onto the inflationary loss. People who had their food stamp allotments cut, for example, also found that whatever stamps they still did get bought fewer groceries week by week and month by month.

Reagan was pleased by the budget-cutting efforts and by his other successes. He had pledged to raise military spending and shore up the nation's defenses, for instance, and he had. Military spending rose by $125 billion between 1981 and 1988. He had promised to cut taxes, especially taxes on corporations, which Reagan and others saw as making it too difficult for American business to grow and expand. Six months into his term, the president signed legislation aimed at producing a tax reduction of $37.6 billion in 1982 and an additional $750 billion over the next five years. In 1986, he signed a tax reform act that placed a lower cap on the amount of tax to be paid by well-to-do individuals and simultaneously removed a few low-income Americans from the tax rolls altogether. He made no headway, however, against the federal deficit. In 1980 Reagan had blamed the $998 billion debt upon reckless spending by past Democratic presidents and Congresses. But by 1986, the national debt had risen to over $2 *trillion*.

Aside from that disappointment, though, Reagan had accomplished economic wonders, he and his admirers said. Thanks to corporate tax cuts, business was thriving, and that meant new jobs.

Unemployment was about 11 percent in 1982, 7 percent in 1986, and two years later, 5.4 percent. In some parts of the country, it was only 2 or 3 percent. Unemployment doesn't go much below that in a capitalist economy, the experts say.

The employed were getting fat paychecks, too. The average worker in manufacturing had watched his or her weekly salary jump from $288.62 at the end of 1980 to $398.75 in April 1987. The inflation rate had slowed, from 13.5 percent a year in 1979 to 2.4 percent nine years later. All-in-all, the president maintained, Americans had every reason to feel happy and confident about the economy and the future.

Mainstream middle- and upper-class America might feel that way, the president's critics responded. What about the rest of the country though? Over twenty-nine million American men, women, and children had been living below the poverty level when Reagan began campaigning for the presidency in 1980. How had welfare cuts, lower tax revenues, higher military outlays, and a growing national debt affected them?

Disastrously—that was the critics' answer. Reagan's policies had amounted to a savage assault upon the welfare systems that serve the nation's poor and near-poor.

It was Michael Harrington who came up with the phrase "savage assault." He used it in a book published in 1987, exactly twenty-five years after *The Other America* had shocked the country and helped pave the way for the War on Poverty.

The New American Poverty

In this book, *The New American Poverty*, Harrington conceded the failure of the War on Poverty. By and large, he attributed that failure to Johnson's obsession with Vietnam, although he saw other factors at work as well. One of the most important, he thought, was the fact that Congress, in enacting its antipoverty legislation, had passed up an opportunity to create a truly national system of welfare. That neglect was not accidental but deliberate.

69

It was a neglect that traced its roots to traditional American attitudes about government involvement in welfare. As we know, such involvement has historically been regarded as socialistic, and therefore bad, and is far more limited in the United States than in either the industrialized democracies of Western Europe or the communist and socialist countries of Eastern Europe. Canada, a country very similar to the United States, also provides its citizens with many more social services than does this country. In addition to old-age pensions, unemployment insurance, and the like, Canadians enjoy guaranteed income supplements to help out when retirement pensions are below a set level; family and youth allowances to all families with children under age fifteen and with sixteen- and seventeen-year-olds who remain in school; and medical and hospital insurance that provides for most health care costs. For decades, the federal government in the Canadian capital of Ottawa has played a leading part in paying for and administering these programs.

Not so the U.S. federal government, whose public welfare role has always been limited. One way Americans have found to do the limiting has been to provide relief at the lowest feasible level of government. First, it was left up to towns and cities to care for their own poor—or not to care for them—as each saw fit. Later, the states began getting involved. Last of all, the national government stepped onto the scene. But even after that happened, it was largely state officials who had the right to decide which of their citizens were eligible for aid and how much should be provided. Congress could have changed that by adopting a single unified system of standards and requirements, but it chose not to. Instead, lawmakers bowed to pressure from "states' righters" who believe states and localities should remain as free as possible from "interference" on the part of the federal officials. The states would continue running their own programs. "So it was—and is—that the United States has fifty-one separate, and quite different, welfare systems (one for each state, plus one for the District of Columbia)," Harrington concluded.

How well were the fifty-one doing in the 1980s? According to the U.S. Bureau of the Census, which keeps tabs on population levels and changes, the twenty-nine million Americans who had been living in poverty in 1980 had grown to over thirty-three million by 1985. That came to 14 percent of the country's total population. Between 1980 and 1982 alone, the poverty rate had increased by 7.4 percent.

Other statistics, too, cast a somewhat different light on the rosy economic picture painted by President Reagan and his backers. An April 1987 paycheck of $398.75, adjusted for inflation, came to only $3 a week more than 1980's $288.62. There were more jobs, but by no means were all of them full-time. A great many had gone to part-time workers such as teenagers, students, and the retired. What was more, in number terms, unemployment had grown along with employment. There were 7.6 million jobless Americans in 1980, compared with 8.2 million in 1986. And that 8.2 million didn't include the thousands of "discouraged unemployed" who had given up looking for work.

Lost Jobs and a New World Economy

Why the unemployment? Harrington believed it had been brought about by a changing world economy. Until the 1970s, the United States had been the global leader in business and industry, with its goods and technology in demand almost everywhere. That demand had kept American factory workers busy and well-paid. But the demand fell off as American goods became more and more expensive.

Their high price was due to a number of factors. The steep cost of American labor was one. Another was that the oil imported from countries like Saudi Arabia and Iran and used to fuel U.S. factories had become so expensive. In 1967 a barrel of oil went for $1.80. In 1980 it was priced at $37.00. U.S. manufacturers had to pass that expense along to those who bought their goods.

Naturally, it wasn't long before the buyers began looking for new trading partners. As U.S. steel prices rose, international consumers turned to cheaper steel from Japan. American steel profits shrank, and mills began shutting down. Japanese automobiles became popular, causing Detroit automakers to fire workers and shut their gates. Inexpensive cloth and clothing from Taiwan and South Korea replaced costly American-made goods; South Korean shoe factories undersold American ones; Japanese television sets, cameras, computers and similar products edged out their American competitors. Between 1981 and 1986, manufacturing slowdowns and plant closings cost 10.8 million men and women their jobs.

Those job losses, many thought, were of greater significance than the job gains of students and others working part-time to earn extra clothes, entertainment, and personal luxuries. The manufacturing and industrial workers laid off in the early 1980s were the adult heads of household with families to support. Close to a third of them were still out of work in 1988. Another third had located new jobs, but had to accept pay cuts of 20 percent or more. Ten percent of the 10.8 million had found only part-time employment.

The job losses will be permanent, Harrington predicted. Some manufacturers regarded the sales slump as cause to shut down their less-profitable factories for good. Others used falling sales as an excuse to automate and to replace human workers with robots or other sophisticated machines. Still others closed their American plants and relocated in places like Mexico, Taiwan, and South Korea, where labor and operating costs were minimal. All this helps explain why, even after the bad times of the early eighties were over and the U.S. economy began to recovery, U.S. factory workers were not rehired for their old jobs. The jobs had simply disappeared.

Other types of jobs had disappeared as well. American farmers were still being pushed off the land by agribusiness, and by the late 1980s, the Middle Western farming belt had the nation's fastest-growing poverty rate. Many farmers left the land with their wives and children to join the urban poor. Of those who continued to cling to family farms, nearly 20 percent had slid below the poverty level. Larry

Baxa, a Kansas corn and sorghum grower, and his three children were among them. "I'm working like a dog and I still don't have any money," Baxa told a *New York Times* reporter in 1987. "The kids aren't getting enough to eat."

There was hunger in Louisiana's oil fields, as well, and in Texas, Oklahoma, Alaska, and Colorado, as jobs in those and other once-booming oil-producing states vanished. The job losses came about when oil prices began dropping from their 1980 high of $37 a barrel. By 1986, the cost of a barrel of crude was down to about $14. Over the six years, oil-industry joblessness climbed 38 percent, throwing thousands of middle-class men and women abruptly into poverty. By the late eighties, the Harold Reid family of Houston, Texas, was struggling to survive on savings and Social Security payments. Before losing his job four years earlier, Reid had been an oil company vice-president with an annual salary of $70,000. He had been bringing home paychecks regularly for forty years.

A different sort of job loss faced Loretta Schwartz-Noble of Pennsylvania. A professional writer, Schwartz-Noble had been divorced, and with divorce a comfortable middle class lifestyle turned into one threatened by poverty. "Suddenly my own security seemed to crumble," she wrote in a book published under the title *Starving in the Shadow of Plenty*. "My children and I had to find a less expensive place to live . . . [in] a poorer and . . . more dangerous part of the city."

Divorce has placed millions of American women and children in similar circumstances. Figures released in 1987 by the Displaced Homemakers Network headquartered in Washington, D.C., suggested there were almost 11.5 million widowed or divorced women in the United States that year, up from just over four million a decade earlier. "Nearly two-thirds of all displaced homemakers have inadequate incomes," the network report stated. About 40 percent existed below the poverty level. As for children, 1988 statistics showed that fully one-fifth of all American youngsters—13 million in all—were living in poverty. One quarter of all those under the age of six were officially

73

considered poor. Two-thirds of U.S. homeless families were headed by a single parent, most often a mother. Schwartz-Noble feared she and her children might become part of those statistics. "The conditions of the people whose lives I had written about suddenly seemed less distant from my own. I was starting to understand how fragile each of our 'secure' positions is," she wrote.

Those words summed up the essence of what people like Harrington meant when they warned of a "new" American poverty. The poverty Americans were seeing in the 1980s was not confined to a few isolated rural or urban pockets, as the 1960s style of poverty-in-the-midst-of-plenty had been. Nor was it limited to certain immigrant groups or to members of racial or ethic minorities or to the uneducated, unskilled, or "just plain lazy." The economic insecurity of the 1980s threatened corporate executives as well as unwed mothers and brawny oilmen along with drug addicts and the ne'er-do-well.

The new American poverty differed from the old in another way. It gave new meaning to the word "homeless."

Homeless Americans

There have always been homeless people, of course—the vagrants of Europe's post-plague years, the American orphans sent west by the Children's Aid Society, the wanderers of the Great Depression. But the American homeless of the 1980s were unlike most of their predecessors. For one thing, there were more of them—up to three million by some reckonings. The highest estimate for depression homelessness is two million. Most of them were single men who, after a few months on the road, would return home to families prepared to help them out in any way they could.

The homeless of the eighties did not have families to go back to, according to Louise Stark of Arizona State University. Often, they *were* families. A 1987 study by a U.S. Conference of Mayors' task force showed that one-third of the nation's homeless that year were families with children. About another third were mentally ill, and frequently drug addicted or physically sick as well. As the 1980s progressed, the nation's streets, parks, and train and bus terminals became "home" to thousands of men and women barely able to care for their most basic needs.

Others among the new homeless included veterans of the war in Vietnam, many of whom had come back to the United States with emotional problems or drug or alcohol addictions. There were teenaged runaways, too. According to the Department of Health and Human Services, more than a million American youngsters leave home each year. Youngest of all the homeless are infants whose mothers abandon them. In 1988, New York City officials were responsible for hundreds of babies left by their mothers in public hospitals. Many of the infants had been born to drug-addicted women and were themselves addicted and suffering the agony of withdrawal symptoms. Others, whose mothers had developed the disease AIDS—Acquired Immune Deficiency Syndrome—were born with the disease. AIDS is invariably fatal, and the life expectancy of these babies is only a few years. In the late eighties, New York City welfare officers were overseeing the care of about 800 homeless AIDS babies.

Behind the flat statistics are real people. One, a woman named Joyce Brown, made headlines after New York Mayor Edward Koch announced a policy of forcing the city's mentally-ill homeless into hospitals. The policy was aimed not only at getting the homeless off the streets but also at helping them. That kind of help wasn't what people like Brown were looking for, though. The forty-year-old former secretary was placed in a psychiatric ward in October 1987. She stayed there three months, during which time she went to court to win the right to refuse mind-altering medication and, in a separate lawsuit, to obtain her release. Eventually, she won both cases. Free of medication, she entered a shelter for the formerly homeless. By May 1988, she was back on the streets, "shouting obscenities and begging for money," as one witness put it. Rehospitalization followed, and eventually an arrest on drug-possession charges.

Joyce Brown was only one of thousands of those caught up in society's probably well-meant, but certainly less-than-successful, attempts to assist the homeless. Many cities had set up public shelters for those with nowhere to live, but despite administrators' best efforts, conditions in most have been deplorable. Cots line the rooms, and the homeless must fight for space. They have to fight for safety, too. Robbery is common in the public shelters, and so is violence, which includes beatings and knifings.

So unsafe are shelters in a number of cities and so limited are their facilities that many of the homeless choose to live elsewhere. A police sergeant in Portland, Maine, told the Associated Press that men there had taken to committing minor crimes so that they would be hauled off to the county jail—with its warm beds and free meals. Finally succumbing to the inevitable, the sheriff opened an emergency shelter right in the jail. Public libraries are other popular hangouts for the homeless. In 1989, officials in Haverhill, Massachusetts, announced plans to include a room designed especially for the homeless in a new library scheduled to open three years later. The room was to be furnished with chairs, sofas, a TV, and a coffeemaker.

Other homeless men and women settle down in train and bus stations. Or in trains themselves. In the spring of 1988, New York City officials allowed a dozen or so homeless men to settle temporarily in a subway car, car No. 4776, to be exact. No. 4776 was part of a work train carrying repairmen and their equipment from one part of the underground system to another. Back and forth the car went, with the men resting on its benches or snoring on the floor. "We're trying to have compassion for these people," one member of the city's Transit Police told a reporter.

Slipping Through the "Safety Net"

Pathetic as these and other addicted, mentally ill, and lonely homeless are, it is easy enough to see how they got the way they are. But what about the one-third of the homeless who are families? How do ordinary working Americans, Americans accustomed to having jobs to go to and places to live and people who love them, slide into homelessness? For thirty-two-year-old David Mirayes of Staten Island, New York, a musician, the fall came after his wife grew ill. Mirayes lost his job when he was forced to quit work to care for her. He slipped behind in his rent and he, his sick wife, and their two children were evicted from their apartment. Turning to the city for help, the family found itself assigned to the Saint George, the welfare hotel we visited back in Chapter 1. After that, Mirayes couldn't work because not only did he still have to care for his wife, but he dared not leave the children alone at the Saint George. Soon after, work became impossible for a third reason—he had to pawn his musical instruments to raise money for food.

Why couldn't David Mirayes locate an adequate apartment for his family? Harrington might say that it is because decent, affordable housing is almost nonexistent for America's poor and near-poor, who barely survive just above the poverty line. He and others lay much of the blame for the lack of housing squarely upon the shoulders of the Reagan administration. This was the administration, after all, that reduced the construction of federally funded low-cost housing by 118,000 units a year. The reduction saved billions of dollars—billions that critics might say probably went to help pay for the massive Reagan defense buildup—but each year the saving translated into thousands upon thousands of families with nowhere to live. In 1987, the U.S. Conference of Mayors studied twenty-six major cities and found that, in two-thirds of them, waiting lists for public housing were so long that officials had stopped accepting new applications.

Harrington would doubtless also fault the administration for the fact that Mirayes had to give up his means of livelihood in order to provide food for his family. In a way, that seems like a stupid move. But what other move could anyone expect a person to make when it's a question of not being able to feed the family because programs like food stamps have been cut? The nutrition spending reductions were politically popular in the early 1980s. Perhaps they helped finance the equally popular federal income tax cuts. But it was left up to the Mirayeses—and to millions of other hungry Americans—to pay the human price for that political triumph. That was how Reagan's critics saw matters, anyway.

In their eyes, the administration's domestic policies had gone awry in another way as well. What about the "safety net" of public and private social services that presidential candidate Reagan had promised? If any public safety net existed, people like Harrington charged, it was a ragged one, with gaps in it large enough for Joyce Brown, the Baxas, the men in subway car No. 4776, and plenty of others to have slipped through.

And private charity wasn't taking up the slack. True, Americans contributed generously to a variety of worthwhile causes throughout the 1980s, giving away $93.68 billion in 1987 alone. Only a small fraction of that giving, however, was directed toward antipoverty programs. Individual charitable donations are more likely to come in the form of college graduates' gifts to an alma mater, contributions to public radio and television, offerings to promote religious work, money given to political parties and candidates, and the like. Corporate charity generally falls into a similar pattern. Business's contribution to the poor looks even smaller when one considers that corporate philanthropy amounted to less than 5 percent of the nation's total donations to charity in 1987.

Even on those occasions when private help is offered to the poor, the giving may not be as charitable as it appears on the surface. A Bozeman, Montana, program singled out by *The Christian Science Monitor* in the late eighties as a high-minded example of "secret" and "temporary" assistance to the town's needy was actually nothing of the sort, one Bozeman resident protested in a letter to the editor. "The private agencies in Bozeman provide a means for those who are unable to survive on the meager state assistance programs in Montana to leave town for an urban center where they are able to receive more substantial assistance," Bob Nichol charged. "The meager charity available in small communities creates and perpetuates *transiency*; it does not assist the poor to rise above their unfortunate circumstances."

Unfair Budget-Cutting?

The final criticism liberals had to make of the welfare budget-cutting was that it had been done in a manner that was deeply unfair. The United States has two separate and distinct types of welfare systems, they say, and while Congress and the administration were hacking fiercely away at one, they were allowing the other to continue to grow and flourish.

One group of U.S. welfare programs is intended to help the poor. These are the programs that most Americans think of when they use the words "welfare" or "relief," programs like AFDC, food stamps, and Medicaid. All are means-tested programs, and anyone who seeks assistance under one of them is required to prove that his or her income is low enough to qualify. But a second group of social welfare programs are non-means-tested. Such programs are open to people regardless of their financial need, and many who benefit from them are not poor at all—but might be if they could not count on these benefits. Examples of non-poverty welfare programs include basic Social Security, Medicare, and guaranteed student loans.

These programs escaped the budget-slashers of the 1980s virtually unscathed, liberals and conservatives agreed. "It's very difficult to get Congress to terminate programs for the middle class," James C. Miller, III, Reagan's director of the Office of Management and Budget, complained in 1988. That's partly because members of the middle and upper classes are more numerous and more powerful than are the needy. They are more likely than the poor to vote in elections; in 1984, three-quarters of Americans with annual incomes over $35,000 went to the polls, compared to fewer than half of those with yearly incomes under $10,000.

Another reason for congressional reluctance to cut into middle-

and upper-class benefits is that most lawmakers are themselves members of the middle and upper class, and they and their families share in benefits aimed at those classes. Even presidents and members of Congress have children and grandchildren who may need guaranteed student loans if they are to attend exclusive private colleges, for instance, and parents for whom Social Security and Medicare mean independence and high-quality health care. State and local officials have families, too. Asking them to cut public spending for middle-class entitlements is asking them to rob themselves and their loved ones. From the start, therefore, social welfare programs enacted by Congress—and by state legislatures as well—have tended to favor the better-off.

Favor to what extent? According to Harrington, federal welfare spending for the poor rose from $4.6 billion to $34.6 billion between 1961 and 1976. That is an increase of $30 billion. During the same years, social spending for the nonpoor rose from $29.4 billion to $196.8 billion. That was an increase of $171.9 billion, almost six times the rise in poverty-program spending. In 1961, 4.7 percent of the federal budget went to help the poor, compared to 9.4 percent for the nonpoor. Fifteen years later, the percentages were 30.1 for the poor, and 54 for the nonpoor.

Of course few well-off Americans think of themselves as the major beneficiaries of the nation's social welfare programs. What do they associate with the word "welfare"? An AFDC mother with eight children and pregnant again. An urban teenager who wants all the good things in life without having to lift a finger to get them. A man under a park bench clutching a bottle. The one kind of person they don't envision when they think of welfare is someone like themselves or their parents or the guy next door. Yet it is precisely those people who draw the greatest benefit from the nation's social welfare spending.

The idea that poor people are the only ones getting anything out of U.S. social welfare systems is one common misconception, liberals say. There are others.

Fraud—Fact or Fiction?

One concerns charges of welfare fraud. Many Americans are convinced that billions of their welfare tax dollars have been funneled off by cheats and chiselers. President Reagan was among them, and his budget-cutting policies grew partly out of his belief that U.S. welfare systems are plagued by "waste, fraud and abuse."

It's natural enough that taxpayers would worry about fraud. They see one person misusing food stamps and wonder if everyone on the stamps does the same. They read about one AFDC mother who collects benefits under two or three different names and addresses and conclude that the practice is widespread. But is it fair to generalize about all relief recipients from a few instances of cheating? Just because one person abuses AFDC or the food stamp program doesn't mean everyone does.

Besides, if you look at things from the point of view of a person on relief, some "fraud" may take on a different coloration. There are food stamp recipients who do try to "beat the system" in order to end up with spare cash. But could it be the system itself that encourages them to act in this way? Think of what people *cannot* buy with food stamps: aspirin, vitamins, toilet paper, tooth paste, laundry soap . . . the list goes on and on. Those products aren't luxuries in our culture; they are necessities.

Sandy, the grocery store clerk we met in Chapter 4, knows that. Irritated as she gets with some of her food stamp customers, she has a lot of sympathy for most others. "One woman came in," she says, "and apologized for her hair looking so awful. She told me she couldn't afford shampoo that week." Sandy has no doubt that was the honest truth. She also knows that if the woman is less than completely scrupulous about how she uses the stamps, it may be because she genuinely needs to lay her hands on all the cash she can.

But the welfare fraud problem goes well beyond petty cheating, many argue. What about the 1987 report from Richard Kusserow of the U.S. Department of Health and Human Services? That report charged that fraud on the part of AFDC mothers had cost the government $1 billion the previous year.

What exactly did Kusserow mean by "fraud," though? "For the sake of clarity," his report stated, "we have used the broader definition of fraud that includes unintentional misrepresentations of facts by clients." In other words, Kusserow was talking about losses resulting from carelessness and honest error as well as those due to deliberate cheating. Critics of his report wondered how clarity was served by any such definition. In *Webster's New Collegiate Dictionary*, the entry under "fraud" reads, in full:

> 1. Deception; deceit; trickery. 2. Artifice; trick. 3. Colloq. A cheat; imposter. 4. Law. An intentional perversion of truth to induce another to part with some valuable thing belonging to him, or to surrender a legal right.—Syn. See DECEPTION; IMPOSTURE.

Not much in that definition about "unintentional misrepresentations of facts." Yet Kusserow's report, and the headlines based on it, gave readers the clear impression that deliberate, calculated fraud on the part of individual AFDC clients was costing the federal government upwards of $1 billion yearly. Actually federal government figures show that charges of cheating are raised in only 3.2 percent of all AFDC cases. In almost half of those cases, the charges are found to be unjustified.

Unjustified or not, the charges have cost a good many welfare clients their benefits. Early in 1986, New York City welfare officials launched a major antifraud offensive. Claims that seemed the least bit dubious were rigorously investigated, and any judged to be fraudulent were denied. As a result, overpayments fell to the lowest level in several decades. That was the good news. The bad was the announcement by the city's Human Resources Administration that many of the claims it had turned down because of suspicion of fraud were actually perfectly legitimate ones. Of the claims denied in 1986, 5.4 percent were denied in error, up from 3.9 percent mistakenly denied the year before. That meant 46,000 honest, eligible men, women, and children were wrongly suspected of fraud and forced off the relief rolls in a single year.

Besides tending to exaggerate cheating by relief recipients (and punishing them, sometimes mistakenly, for it), Americans may overlook less-than-honest behavior on the part of others who have dealings with the nation's welfare systems. What others, for instance? Welfare hotel landlords come to mind. Charging exorbitant rates for filthy, rat-infested firetraps of rooms may not be illegal, but it certainly must be rated unethical.

Other nonrecipients who squeeze a little extra profit out of the nation's welfare systems may include hospital administrators and doctors who overcharge government for their Medicare patients. A 1988 report by HHS's Kusserow showed that mistakes crop up in 20 percent of all Medicare hospital claims. Over 60 percent of the time, the errors favor the hospital. They were, the report said, costing the federal government several hundred million dollars a year. In a separate report issued at the same time, Kusserow charged that about 10 percent of Medicare hospital admissions were "not medically justified." Another loss to the taxpaying public. Still another was revealed the same year by the U.S. Attorney General's office. Close to a thousand Pennsylvania and New Jersey physicians had received an average of $523 in a Medicare kickback scheme, Assistant U.S. Attorney James G. Sheehan charged. About a hundred of them got more than $5,000 each. Altogether, HHS figures show, Medicare is overcharged to the tune of $2 billion annually.

But of all the welfare frauds around, none has been more outrageous than the one Americans began learning about in the spring and summer of 1989. The scandal in the federal Department of Housing and Urban Development included incidents of theft, bribery, and the for-profit appropriation by public officials and their families of housing intended for low-income Americans. At least two Reagan administration federal department heads were implicated in the affair, and so were a number of other leading Republican party members, such as former Senator Edward Brooke of Massachusetts and Paul Manafort, campaign advisor to President Reagan and Vice-President (by then President) George Bush. Twenty million dollars—maybe more—was spirited away by various people working at or with HUD. One Baltimore woman stole $5.5 million between 1985 and 1988. No one at HUD cared what she was doing—or even noticed. "It's a circus," she said of the agency. "Cesspool" was *The New York Times*'s word for it. And all this in a department whose funding had already been halved by an administration determined to root out waste, fraud, and mismanagement in social welfare spending!

Needless to say, the fact that some hospital administrators, doctors, slumlords, and others may abuse the nation's social welfare systems does not excuse individual poverty-program recipients who also cheat. But before people lump all relief recipients together and condemn them as cheats, they might reflect upon the fact that not only is the amount of recipient fraud frequently overstated, but it is also far from being the only kind of dishonesty in the system.

Other Welfare Myths

Other misconceptions about antipoverty programs, many say, relate to the type of people who depend on them. According to popular belief, large numbers of those on relief are ablebodied men who could perfectly well get jobs if they wanted to. But government figures indicate that only about 1 percent of those on welfare fall into that category. About a third of all recipients are children. Another 20 percent or so are displaced homemakers.

Prejudices about AFDC mothers are generally unfair, too, many say. In the public imagination, these mothers have enormous families and are constantly pregnant. Most often, they are black. They have no desire to work or try to better themselves.

Even the briefest look at AFDC statistics shows how mistaken that image is. The majority of AFDC mothers (like the majority of relief recipients overall) are white. Two-thirds of them have only one or two children; fewer than 14 percent have four or more. About a third of AFDC mothers stay in the program more than eight years, but another third manage to leave it in less than two. Nor is it true that large numbers of girls and women have one illegitimate child after another for the purpose of getting increased AFDC benefits. According to the one study, the percentage of illegitimate births increased less rapidly among AFDC mothers than among the population at large throughout the 1970s.

Still another misconception is that the welfare lifestyle is easier and more comfortable than the lifestyle of the working poor. In some ways, it is. Certainly the welfare mother New York's Mayor Koch wrote about in *The New York Times* was financially better off on relief than she would have been off it. But there's more to life than finances. At about the time the mayor's article came out, another city woman, this one determined to avoid welfare, appeared on a television news program to talk about her life. The woman was married, the mother of a three-year-old, and pregnant. Both she and her husband were employed full time, but since their daughter was chronically ill with asthma and needed hundreds of dollars' worth of medical care each month, even their combined incomes left them in desperate straits. Wouldn't the family fare better if the mother, and perhaps the father, too, quit working and applied for Medicaid and other public benefits? the reporter demanded. Yes, the mother replied, but that was not going to happen. Anything would be preferable to life on welfare.

What's It Like to Ask for Help?

A lot of America's poor and near-poor think the same—and with good reason. For many, the first reason is the humiliation of having to ask for public assistance to begin with. Affluent people are not the only ones who believe in the work ethic and the value of independence and self-sufficiency. A laid-off Texas oil-rig dismantler burst into tears as he signed his first-ever set of unemployment compensation papers in 1987. "My parents raised me to believe . . . you make your own way," he said.

Retirees who have spent their entire lives working may feel the same way. A 1988 congressional study showed that only half of the nation's most destitute—here defined as its elderly, blind, and disabled—were taking advantage of a supplementary, means-tested Social Security program for which they were eligible. Many who refuse to apply for benefits refuse "because of the stigma of welfare," according to *The New York Times.*

When people do overcome their reluctance and request assistance, there may be difficulties in the way of getting it. We've already seen how antifraud efforts cut into the benefits of the eligible, but there are other impediments as well. Welfare applicants often have to stand in long lines to have their papers processed. For some, a language barrier exists. The officials with whom they deal may be rushed and insensitive at best, rude or even cruel at worst. The elderly, who may be hard-of-hearing or have other physical handicaps, find it especially difficult to deal with this aspect of going on welfare. People of all ages find that embarrassing questions may be asked—and have to be answered—in public. They may be made to feel like second-class citizens.

Even with the application process complete, help that is both needed and deserved may not be forthcoming. In her book *Starving in the Shadow of Plenty*, Loretta Schwartz-Nobel reported a conversation with one woman waiting in a public aid office. "For six months I haven't been able to get food stamps or money," the woman told her. "I'm about to have my electricity and gas cut off. I have no money. I have no food and I have no food stamps. I have received a notice that I must move, but I have no place to go." Asked how she got into this fix, the woman explained that it had come about because of a bureaucratic mixup. "Somehow it seems that I got on the wrong mailing list," she explained. "Nobody knows why I have been cut off and nobody knows how to get me back on. Every time I come here they tell me they're still working on it."

Perhaps they were working with a computer. Perhaps that was the problem. In March 1987 a new computer system, one that was supposed to simplify the welfare process, was put into place by New York City's Human Resources Administration. Over the next nine months, this "state of the art" system delayed benefits to thousands. Some received no payments at all for the rest of the year. One who did not, a mother of three named Maria Santiago, complained to a news reporter about her situation. "I do not understand the problems," she told him. "I feel cheated." She showed the reporter a note from the Human Resources Administration: "The recipient had a medical emergency but we are unable to issue a Medicaid card at this time because the case has not yet been entered into the Medicaid computer files."

The Santiagos had other problems. Deprived of benefits, the family had been forced into a shelter for the homeless and was still living there. Lots of other city welfare recipients whose benefits had been mistakenly cut off were in shelters as well. According to a 1987 report by Dr. Anna Lou Dehavenon of the Human Resources Administration, about half of those then seeking emergency shelter had to do so within two months of their payments being stopped. It was *because* those payments were stopped that they could no longer afford rent. Once having given up their homes, they had little hope of finding new ones in the same rent range. Affordable housing for the poor hardly exists in American towns and cities. "The Human Resources Administration creates some of the problems it's supposed to solve for the homeless and other low-income families," Dehavenon acknowledged.

There are other frustrations connected with being on relief and more than just bureaucratic bumbling or misplaced suspicions of fraud that stand in the way of people's getting the help to which they have a legal right. In some cases, the very government officials charged with administering that help seem determined for philosophical or political reasons to do all they can to prevent its being given out. Take the controversy that engulfed the Women, Infants and Children (WIC) program in the 1970s as an example.

WIC was established as a means-tested nutrition program aimed at needy pregnant and nursing women, their babies, and children under age four. In September 1972 Congress approved $40 million in WIC funds to be disbursed through the U.S. Department of Agriculture over the next two years. The plan was for department officials to award cash grants to the states, which would then turn the money over to local agencies. But the head of the department, Earl Butz, was reluctant to carry out the congressional mandate. Named to his post by President Richard Nixon, Butz, like Nixon, was a conservative and a sharp critic of "handout" programs. First, he and other department officials engaged in foot-dragging claims that the department was "not organized to undertake" the medical testing that would indicate whether or not the program was providing a needed and adequate level of nutrition. This point was debated for five months, during which time no WIC funds were made available to the poor. Finally the Department of Agriculture agreed to design a "small, statistically valid medical evaluation" of the program. The $40 million appropriated by Congress would pay for this study, they added.

At that, angry advocates for the needy brought the department to court. In August 1973, a judge ordered the money spent, as Congress had ordered, on food for hungry women and children. Agriculture officials complied, but a new controversy cropped up the next year when they ordered blood tests on WIC babies and children. The tests themselves were not the problem—they could be useful in determining whether or not the food supplements were actually improving recipients' health. The trouble was that the blood samples were to be drawn from each youngster's jugular, the large vein in the neck that carries blood from the head back to the heart. "A trade-off of blood for food" the Children's Foundation of Washington, D.C., called that directive. To one Detroit doctor and city council member, Mary Ann Mahaffey, such testing "smacked of experimentation" on the poor. "Such tests are not only dangerous to infants but they also discourage hungry people from participating in the program," she claimed. Perhaps that sense of discouragement was exactly what the Department of Agriculture was trying to promote.

It wasn't long before the jugular directive was withdrawn, but WIC's troubles were not yet over. Some states were displaying little more eagerness to implement its programs than was the federal government. In 1980, Pennsylvania officials blamed a malfunctioning computer for an error that resulted in thousands of eligible women and children being denied their WIC benefits. Once the error was discovered, the officials waited ten months to correct it. Ten months, with women and children going hungry in the depressed months of the early eighties. Eventually, $8.5 million in unspent Pennsylvania WIC funds had to be returned to the U.S. Treasury. Because of the way the WIC law was written, the money could not be recovered and spent on Pennsylvania's needy.

When allowed to function as intended, however, WIC has functioned well. A study released in 1986 showed that babies of WIC mothers are born larger, healthier, and with fewer birth defects than those of poor women outside the program. The number of stillbirths and the infant death rate are lower among WIC than non-WIC mothers, too. Another study, this one conducted by the federal Centers for Disease Control, concluded that the rate of anemia in WIC children dropped by two-thirds between 1975 and 1985.

Nevertheless, WIC continues to encounter problems. By 1988, the program was serving only 44 percent of those who qualified for it. That year, the Senate turned down a proposal to increase WIC spending by $150 million a year. The increase, if approved, would have brought an additional 4 percent of America's poverty-level women and children into the program. The Senate, however, limited the increase to $48 million.

More Frustrations

Other welfare rules and regulations serve to frustrate the poor. A Boston man who signed his name "Michael D." wrote about his dilemma in a local newspaper. "I have been unemployed for fourteen weeks. I would like to train to be a cook . . . Massachusetts . . . has a seventeen-week, full-time, basic orientation course (with a living stipend), for people who want to become cooking professionals. Now here's the catch: You have to be unemployed for fifteen weeks to qualify. The course starts at a given time. If you don't start at the beginning, you have to wait another seventeen weeks to be eligible. I can't afford to remain unemployed any longer. Is this crazy bureaucracy or what?"

Another who ran into roadblocks in the welfare system was Joni Manning. In 1988, Joni was living at the Larchmont Motel, a welfare hotel in Westchester County, New York, with her five-year-old daughter. She searched the classified ads daily in search of an apartment, and each time she found one, she phoned the owners and left a message asking them to call back. None did. "You leave your number, and as soon as they call and hear 'Larchmont Motel,' that's the end of it." Owners of rental units don't want welfare-hotel-type people—whatever that "type" is—in their property. Joni ran into a similar problem when she went looking for work. A job interview with one woman, she said, "was fine until I handed her my resume and it said 1361 Boston Post Road. Everyone in this town knows 1361 Boston Post Road." It's the Larchmont's address.

Even if Joni does manage to find work, her problems won't be over. Who will take care of her daughter? Affordable day care is in terribly short supply in the United States. In New York City, public quality day care is available to only 36 percent of eligible preschoolers, and to no more than 6 percent of eligible infants and toddlers. For New York welfare mothers, one answer to the day care problem could be to train continually for jobs they never take. New York state does provide some child care for women in job-training programs. Once they leave the program and start looking for work, though, the service is no longer available.

Another day-care solution to which thousands of desperate

mothers have started turning is the local public library. The parents of "about two thousand children" are "using the library as an after-school child-care center," Penny Markey of the Los Angeles County library system told an Associated Press reporter in 1988. In New York, children as young as two or three are dropped off at libraries in the morning and picked up there at night. Chicago librarian Helen Goodman complained that her once-quiet book stacks now resemble "scenes of the stock exchange that they show on television." She doesn't like to turn children away, but she is aware that she and other librarians are not only inappropriate as day care providers, but also inadequate. Safety is one reason. At a branch library in Brooklyn, New York, officials tell of members of street gangs roaming through the building snatching jewelry. During one month alone, Brooklyn police made four crack arrests in the children's room.

Of course, when Joni's daughter begins school, a big chunk of the day care problem will be solved. If she starts school, that is. The obstacles in her way could be considerable. Ten-year-old Novena Simmons spent the 1987-88 school year commuting 120 miles a day between her school and the Westchester County welfare hotel where she lived with her mother. In New York City, one welfare mother had to sacrifice four of her precious dollars every day to provide transportation for her two children to and from school. New York City public school students of all income levels are routinely issued public transit passes, but a snafu in the welfare bureaucracy kept these particular children from getting theirs.

For many families, the sacrifices involved in getting an education are just too great. Nationwide, at least 42 percent of homeless children were not attending school in 1988, according to a review conducted by Travelers Aid International. In New York City, the homeless student nonenrollment figure was 50 percent. The reasons children skip school go beyond problems of transportation: they may be too sick or hungry to go to classes or to perform adequately there. They may find it impossible to complete homework assignments or study for tests. A

91

child who lives with two other people in a chairless, tableless, nine-by twelve-foot space—as is often the case—is going to experience a certain amount of difficulty doing either. Truants may be missing school because of lack of decent clothes or shoes. They may be psychologically unequipped to stand up to teasing from the children of better-off families or to subtle belittlement from unsympathetic teachers. What kind of welfare system, the critics ask, would permit the existence of conditions that virtually ensure its children will grow up uneducated and unskilled? Isn't that just asking for welfare dependency to extend into coming generations?

Saving Money or Increasing Dependency?

Nor is it only youngsters on welfare who find the road to education and job skills blocked. Public assistance programs in many states and cities have been geared more toward requiring recipients to find jobs than toward teaching them to do jobs. That's partly because the federal spending cuts of the 1980s meant reduced funding for education and manpower training. But it's also due to the fact that in many states and localities officials have traditionally undertaken to compel welfare recipients to take jobs—any jobs at all—in order to get them off relief.

For thousands of poor people, the two combine to force them to settle for minimum-wage or part-time work instead of job training or further education. Forcing a welfare recipient to chose unskilled minimum-wage work over investing in his or her future through education or vocational training doesn't really promote self-sufficiency, many say. It just about guarantees that there will be a new period of dependency in the future. Work requirements and education cutbacks saved the nation some money in the short term, they add, but both could prove costly in the long run.

In other welfare areas, too, saving money in one way can mean squandering it in others. Take the housing situation. Putting up a homeless family in a place like the Larchmont Motel costs $1,950 a month for a single room. That's an amount that adds up quickly,

Mamaroneck Town Supervisor Dolores Battalia told *The New York Times.* "Some people at [the Larchmont] have been there long enough that you could have bought them a whole house." But the county can't. The money with which it pays its Larchmont bills can legally be used only to provide emergency temporary shelter. Without state and federal subsidies, Westchester officials cannot build low-cost public housing. "And," said a spokesman for the county's Department of Social Services, "the federal government and the state . . . have essentially been out of this business for several years." Apparently, some HUD officials had gone into the corruption business instead.

Larchmont residents can't even save the county money by moving into an apartment. For a family of four on welfare, the rental allowance is no more than $393 a month. That's not enough to rent a place in expensive Westchester County. Of course the rental allowance could be increased—to $950 a month, say—and still save taxpayers $1,000 monthly. But so far that hasn't happened. "Illogical" is how one Westchester welfare official characterizes the situation.

"Illogical" is the word for more than welfare housing policies. Novena Simmons was doing her daily school commute in a taxi, with the county picking up the tab. A hundred and twenty miles a day in a *taxi?* Novena had no choice; public transportation is limited in Westchester, and her school district was sixty miles from the hotel to which the county assigned her and her mother.

Novena's daily taxi rides were more than a simple waste of money. They were also part of the reason mainstream American taxpayers feel so much resentment toward those on welfare. No one in his or her right mind could help feeling that there is something awfully wrong about spending so much money to get a ten-year-old to and from classes—and that includes the Simmonses. They weren't any happier about all that money being spent than were their taxpaying fellow citizens. It's not as if the money was going to them personally. They knew that county residents must have resented the taxi bill—resented Novena for running it up. And they weren't happy about Novena doing all that traveling, either. The child was so exhausted when she came home every day that she could hardly do her homework and so tired by each morning trip that she forgot most of what she had learned by the time school was reached. But what were Novena and her mother supposed to do? They were powerless to change county welfare policies.

They, and the rest of the nation's thirty-three million poor are powerless to change other illogical policies, practices, and attitudes. Powerless to change a system that keeps almost half of all homeless children out of school and thwarts a Joni Manning or a Michael D. who wants to work or train for a job. Powerless to alter the thinking of those who condemn AFDC mothers for not working while denying them child care and job training. Powerless to keep public officials from ordering blood drawn from the jugulars of infants. Powerless to raise WIC funding to cover even half of those eligible for the program. Powerless to keep those excluded from the program from running the risk of bearing unhealthy children, children with a better-than-average chance of growing up sickly, handicapped, or mentally retarded—a burden on society for years to come.

But if America's poor are powerless to change the system, others—members of Congress and the state legislatures, for example—are not. And as the 1980s wound down, change was in the air.

6

Making Changes

Talk of welfare reform was nothing new in 1988. By then, the discussion had been going on for close to twenty years.

Among those who helped begin it was Richard Nixon. Already, when Nixon was elected president in November 1968, it was becoming obvious that Lyndon Johnson's War on Poverty was not, after all, going to transform the United States into the Great Society. On August 8 of the next year, Nixon went on nationwide radio and television to speak to the American people about the nation's relief system—and to present his own plan for welfare reform. He called the proposal the Family Assistance Plan—FAP for short.

Under FAP, the president informed listeners and viewers, AFDC would be eliminated. In its place would be a federally guaranteed minimum income allowance. This allowance would amount to $1,600 a year for a family of four. It would be paid, not only to the jobless and indigent, but to working people whose annual income came to less than $2,320 per four-member family.

At first, the Nixon plan seemed to have something for everyone— and a good chance of getting through Congress. Liberals liked the guaranteed minimum income provision because of what it would do to help raise the living standard of the very poorest, especially in the rural South. They also approved its similarity to another scheme many of them favored: the so-called negative income tax. Under the negative income tax, people on relief would lose only fifty cents in benefits for every dollar they earned above a certain minimum level.

Liberals also applauded the fact that the wage guarantee was to come from the federal government rather than from the states. For years they had been pushing for a stronger federal role in welfare, arguing that state-to-state discrepancies in benefit levels, eligibility requirements, and so on made traditional U.S. relief systems unfair. Finally, liberals were glad to see two-parent families, including working families, included under FAP. Here, for a change, was a program designed to help parents and children stay together. One criticism of AFDC had always been that it tended to break families up, forcing fathers (and sometimes mothers) to desert their children so those children could qualify for payments. And by supplementing the incomes of men and women with the lowest-paid jobs, FAP would encourage people to keep those jobs instead of exchanging them for the greater monetary benefits of life on welfare.

Conservatives discovered much to approve in the Nixon program as well. One thing they liked was the provision that under some circumstances FAP participants could be removed from the program at the discretion of welfare officials. No longer would recipients be automatically entitled to a hearing at which they could defend their right to remain on the relief rolls. Conservatives were also pleased to note that anyone in FAP deemed "suitable" for employment would have to take a job, even if that job paid less than the minimum wage. This work-for-welfare, or "workfare," idea has generally been popular with those most adamant about people on welfare being forced to earn their keep.

Yet conservatives weren't completely satisfied with the Nixon proposal. Providing a minimum income for the poor and near-poor would be an expensive proposition, many pointed out—one that could be counted on to grow over time. Besides, how could the citizens of a capitalist nation seriously consider putting the federal government in the position of guaranteeing everyone a living? Capitalism is supposed to be about independence and competition, not about security and guarantees. To people like financial writer Henry Hazlitt, the guaranteed income idea seemed a perilous step toward the welfare state and socialism. It is "wrong in principle," Hazlitt wrote, to allow government to forcibly seize money from those who work and give it to those who don't simply because the latter don't have money. Still another concern centered on the plan's workfare provision. Was it strict enough or would welfare recipients continue to take from society while giving little or nothing back? Conservative opposition to the Nixon reform package was beginning to take root.

So was liberal opposition. What conservatives liked about FAP, liberals didn't. The workfare idea was too harsh, they said, meant to discourage the needy from applying for welfare and making it as unpleasant as possible for them to stay on it. Permitting welfare officials to remove recipients from the rolls almost at will, and denying those so removed the right to speak up for themselves, would result in thousands being taken off welfare prematurely and unjustly. Nor was a $1,600 a year minimum income enough for a family of four. The income threshold would need to be higher, liberals said. The more they thought about the Nixon welfare plan, the less appealing it seemed.

It was the same for conservatives—and eventually even for Nixon himself. Over the months, the president backed away from his proposal and eventually abandoned it altogether. FAP was finished.

Other Reform Ideas

But talk of some other kind of welfare reform was not. Everyone, it appeared, had suggestions for change. Henry Hazlitt did, and he outlined them in his 1973 book, *The Conquest of Poverty*. One Hazlitt proposal was to stop offering relief in the form of outright cash payments like AFDC or WIC vouchers or food stamps. Make welfare available on a loan basis instead, he urged. Not as a loan that recipients *must* repay when they go off welfare, but one that they *may* repay if they choose to.

What repayment incentive was Hazlitt suggesting? Restoration of a former recipient's right to vote. Depriving everyone on welfare of that right was another of Hazitt's reform ideas. Keeping welfare recipients away from the ballot box was "practically imperative" if the nation were to solve its welfare dilemma, he wrote. When welfare recipients do vote, after all, they vote for their own interests—in favor of more generous benefits. Limit the right to vote to the self-supporting and to those former welfare recipients who have repaid their debt to society, and the nation's welfare bill will plummet.

Controversial as Hazlitt's proposals were, they hardly compared in that respect to the welfare reform proposal put forth by William Shockley, a professor at Stanford University in California and one of three winners of the 1956 Nobel Prize in physics. Shockley earned his share in the prize for his work on the invention of the transistors used in electronic equipment, but he fancied himself as an expert on human intelligence and race.

It was Shockley's theory—a theory that contradicts all actual scientific evidence—that black children and adults are less intelligent than white. Furthermore, he contended, again in the face of over-whelming scientific data to the contrary, blacks inevitably pass their mental inferiority on from one generation to the next. These "facts" explained, to Shockley's satisfaction at least, why blacks, who make up just over 12 percent of the overall U.S. population, account for a much greater percentage of the welfare population. Blacks, in his view, just aren't bright enough to compete successfully in a capitalist society. And the same "facts" seemed to him to point toward a way to cut the nation's welfare rolls: keep blacks from increasing their numbers by having children. Shockley's idea was to offer blacks cash if they would allow themselves to be sterilized. The cash would be offered on a sliding scale. Black adults would be tested for intelligence, and the lower their scores, the more money they would get in return for sterilization.

Ugly, racist, and unscientific as this proposal was, Shockley was not alone in making it. One of President Nixon's assistants, a man named Roger Freeman, also recommended replacing welfare with sterilization. Freeman proposed a program of "birth prevention" for the poor, again in the form of cash for anyone who agreed to forfeit forever his or her chance to have children. In addition, Freeman wanted Congress to authorize government officials to take some welfare youngsters away from their mothers and raise them in "well-run" government institutions.

To many other Americans, of course, such welfare reform ideas seemed monstrous. Well-run government institutions? Shades of England's nineteenth-century workhouses, they cried. Most liberals and middle-of-the-roaders and a great many conservatives shared their revulsion for ideas like those expressed by Freeman and Shockley. But what other direction could reform take?

George McGovern, at that time a U.S. Senator from South Dakota, thought he knew. In 1972, members of the Democratic party picked McGovern to run for president against Richard Nixon, who was hoping for a second term in office. Welfare reform was one campaign issue, with McGovern promising to implement a federally guaranteed minimum income or a negative income tax—but at a much higher level than Nixon had proposed three years earlier.

That promise was quickly laughed off the political stage. How did his rival think the federal government could even begin paying for such a program? Nixon demanded. Pressed for convincing financial predictions, McGovern came up woefully short on details. Nixon won in a landslide.

For a time after that, little was heard about welfare reform. Then, in 1976, Democrat Jimmy Carter was elected president and started work on a reform plan on his own. Two years later he presented it to the nation.

Again, the plan involved a trade-off of work for welfare. And again it failed in Congress. Congressional liberals objected to the president's proposal that most relief recipients be classified as "expected to work." The provision was cruel and unnecessary and discriminated against the mothers of young children, they protested. Conservatives didn't like the idea that many of the jobs recipients would be "expected" to fill would be public service jobs created at taxpayer expense by the federal government. What was wrong with poor people going out and taking any minimum-wage—or less than minimum-wage—job they could find in the private sector? conservatives wanted to know. Stalemate. "Welfare reform is dead," William P. Albrecht, associate professor of economics at the University of Iowa, told a group in 1980. *"Welfare reform will not be enacted by Congress; it is politically impossible . . ."*

Impossible—or Essential?

Not everyone agreed. Some in Congress and around the country continued to regard reform not only as possible but also as essential. And if they thought it essential in 1980, the year Ronald Reagan was elected to the White House pledging massive cuts in antipoverty programs, it seemed even more crucial eight years later. By then, Americans were waking up to the devastating effect those cuts had had on the nation's poor. Attitudes were changing again, and as the 1990s approached, people began expressing a renewed willingness to help their fellow citizens in need—but only if that help were administered through a new and better system. Their feelings were made clear by a poll showing that when asked if they favored more spending on welfare, an overwhelming majority answered "no." When "welfare" was changed to "assistance to the poor," they answered "yes" by an equally wide margin.

So Congress and the country started talking welfare reform again. One reform plan—a plan journalists promptly labeled "daring" and "bold"—came in 1988 from David T. Ellwood, an economics professor at Harvard University. Ellwood outlined his ideas in a book, *Poor Support: Poverty in the American Family.*

The plan had five major parts. In the first place, Ellwood called for a program to guarantee basic medical care for all Americans. The program, like health-care programs in Canada and Europe, would be paid for and administered through the federal government.

Getting such a medical system in place in the United States was vitally important, Ellwood argued, because modern medicine is so complex and costs so much that millions of Americans are economically unequipped to handle the expense of a single serious illness. Not just Americans living below the poverty line, either. The working-class parents of an asthmatic child may have to choose between struggling to barely provide for that child's health needs and quitting their jobs and going on welfare in order to qualify for Medicaid. We saw an example of such a family in Chapter 5. Even an affluent professional man or woman would be hard pressed to pay the bills for a major medical procedure like an organ transplant or to support someone with a condition as devastating as AIDS. Although just about all professionals, and millions of other working Americans as well, are enrolled in health insurance programs, the insurance rarely pays the full cost of such diseases or procedures. Some medical situations are not covered at all. What's more, many families lack health insurance entirely, either because they cannot afford it or because it is not offered through their place of employment.

The nation's elderly are at special economic risk when ill health strikes. Thousands, even among those covered by Medicare, have watched everything they worked for and saved over the years wiped out by a catastrophic illness. More thousands have found themselves unable to afford the long-term nursing or nursing home care they must have if they are to go on living, let alone go on living in any kind of comfort. Only if the federal government provides a minimum level of medical coverage, Ellwood wrote, will the poor, the working poor, and even much of the middle class be protected against unexpected overnight disaster.

The professor's second proposal was for an increase in the minimum wage. When his book was published in mid-1988, the federal minimum was $3.35 an hour, not enough to provide for the needs of most families. Unless those needs are provided for, what is the point of working? Independence, self-sufficiency, and respect for the traditional American work ethic are all very well, but people can't eat them or use them to clothe their children or to put a roof over their heads. Food, clothing, and shelter are available only in exchange for cold cash. Wouldn't it be better to offer that cash by means of a higher minimum wage than through a handout program? That way, we might see fewer people like the AFDC mother Mayor Edward Koch berated in his 1988 piece in *The New York Times.* If that woman could have located a decently paying job, she might have been able to give her children a sense of independence and the value of work *and* that large color television.

Thirdly, Ellwood proposed forcing parents to support their children—even if they have run off and abandoned those children. How? Identify both parents of each child, he suggested, and list their Social Security numbers on that child's birth certificate. This permanent record would allow government officials to put their hands on all absent working parents, no matter how far away they move or how hard they try to hide. Then those officials could take legal action to ensure that each parent contributes a "reasonable" portion of his or her wages toward the child's upkeep. In the case of a child whose parent could not be traced because he or she had no job or for some other reason, the government itself would have to be responsible for providing a minimum level of support. This one element of Professor Ellwood's plan alone promised to save U.S. taxpayers billions of AFDC dollars every year.

The next portion of Ellwood's program was more radical. His suggestion: change, for the first time in over half a century, the fundamental thrust of the nation's antipoverty programs.

Changing the Way Welfare Works

Originally, back when the stock market crashed and the Great Depression began, people thought of public assistance as a means of helping the unfortunate through a crisis. Relief was offered on a short-term basis, giving the neediest a boost and affording them the chance to get back on their feet financially. With programs like Aid to Dependent Children, though, the system switched direction, gradually offering more and more long-term support to more and more people.

Why? In part, perhaps, because to some, life on public assistance seemed easier and more pleasant than life off it. But wasn't it the system itself that made the welfare lifestyle the only alternative in many cases? That system had come to resemble a sticky tar baby, attracting the needy and luring them into it with all sorts of promises, then trapping them in a deepening cycle of poverty, helplessness, despair—and more poverty. Think of people like Westchester's Joni Manning, unable to find work because her welfare-hotel address made employers unwilling to hire her; unable to move out of the hotel because public low-rental units were unavailable and because her address made private landlords wary; and unable in any event to have taken a job because no day care was available for her daughter. Or of Novena Simmons, whose schoolroom gains were practically canceled out by her exhausting 120-mile-a-day commute. Or of Michael D. from Boston whose desire for job training was blocked by the very welfare bureaucracy he was trying to escape. All three, and their families, too, seemed doomed by the system to stay within it.

So why not change the system back? Ellwood asked. Make public assistance a temporary, short-term affair again. Allow a needy person to be on relief for eighteen to thirty-six months, no more.

But make those months count, he added. Make them a time of "serious . . . financial, educational, and social support." Stop trying to save a few welfare dollars by slashing nutrition spending and public housing budgets. Welfare hotels and semistarvation are destructive both of people's health and of their sense of physical and mental well-being. The sick and depressed are not nearly as well equipped to pull themselves out of poverty as are the mentally and physically sound. Stop cutting corners on school programs, job training, and counselling services. The uneducated and unskilled have small chance of competing or excelling in today's tough job market. If government officials and the public genuinely want men and women to get off relief and into the workforce, they must equip them with the tools to do so. Stop enforcing "Mickey Mouse" rules and resorting to complex and bizarre regulations aimed at discouraging people from even applying for welfare. Help them instead to find jobs and develop feelings of self-worth. That, Ellwood contended, will allow the great majority to make the transition from welfare dependency to long-term self-sufficiency in relatively short order.

Of course the system won't work for everyone. There will always be some people so physically, mentally, or emotionally handicapped that they must fall back upon society in order to survive. Others will be unable for one reason or another to learn a marketable skill or hold a job in the regular workplace. Some will be antisocial or lazy and unmotivated. Ellwood recognized that such people exist and always will, and to them, he thought, the federal government must continue to hold out a helping hand. Job programs like the old Civilian Conservation Corps or the Works Projects Administration of the 1930s could be revived, keeping thousands busy at the minimum wage, for instance. Government-sponsored employment in private business and industry would enable others to support themselves. Establishing the federal government as the employer of last resort was the fifth and final part of Ellwood's antipoverty proposal.

Like any other public policy proposal, Ellwood's came in for criticism. It should come as no surprise that one of the first issues raised was the program's cost, which Ellwood estimated at somewhere between $20 and $30 billion over the first five years. That estimate put the program "beyond the pale," according to Leslie Lenkowsky, of the American Enterprise Institute, a conservative Washington, D.C., "think tank." The huge price tag was probably the largest single factor in the characterization of Ellwood's program as bold and daring.

Lenkowsky and others further suspected that Ellwood's money

estimate was too low and that his program would actually turn out to cost taxpayers even more than $5 or $6 billion a year. The professor was assuming, for instance, most people would make the transition from welfare status to independence quickly and that the number of those requiring aid beyond the eighteen- to thirty-six-month limit would be small. Conservatives tended to come to the opposite conclusion—that the number would be large. "Serious" temporary relief would prove so attractive to recipients that they would do anything so they could stay on it, they predicted. Or rather, they would refuse to do anything—like work—that would take them off it. Welfare people "don't respond to incentives" like job training and educational opportunities, Lawrence Mead, a political scientist at New York University, charged. And what about estimated medical expenses under the plan's guaranteed health-care provisions? With doctor and hospital costs soaring at their present rates, taxpayers could find themselves facing an enormous bill.

Professor Mead objected to Ellwood's program on other grounds, particularly on the government-as-employer-of-last-resort idea. Government is in place to govern, not to provide make-work for the unemployable or shiftless, many say.

The Minimum Wage Issue

Ellwood also came in for criticism over his proposal to increase the minimum wage. The minimum wage law has been a bone of contention in the United States since Congress enacted its original measure in 1938. That law, incidentally, went into effect nearly fifty years after New Zealand became the first nation in the world to adopt minimum wage legislation. The basic pay scale set by Congress in 1938 was twenty-five cents an hour, but the rate applied only to a small number of workers in industries that conducted business across state lines. The law has been rewritten and broadened several times since then, and by the late 1980s it covered close to 60 million workers, most of whom were earning well above the minimum. Support for the minimum wage—and for raising it—has always been strongest among Democrats and labor union members, while opposition has come chiefly from conservatives and people in the business community.

Some people advocate doing away with the minimum wage entirely. That in itself would constitute a hefty contribution toward welfare reform, they say. Those who think this way argue that enforcing a minimum wage keeps some people, especially poor people with few job skills, from finding work. Employers are simply not willing to pay $3.35 an hour to someone barely able to perform even the most menial labor. They might, however, be willing to pay that same person $1.50 or $2.00 an hour. Keeping the minimum wage low, or eliminating it outright, would therefore mean more employment opportunities for the very people who need them most. That would, in turn, mean relief for the country's overburdened welfare systems. Raising the minimum, on the other hand, will lead to job losses. Figures issued in 1988 by the U.S. Department of Labor tended to support this point of view. According to department estimates, each 10 percent increase in the minimum wage means 100,000 to 200,000 lost jobs.

Nevertheless, in 1989, Congress did vote to raise the minimum wage, first to $3.80 per hour effective in April 1990, then to $4.25 an hour in 1991. President Bush signed the act.

So one part of Ellwood's welfare reform proposal did become reality within months of his making it. Another part seemed fated to do the same. In May 1988, Congress enacted the first-ever major expansion of Medicare, voting to insure 32 million elderly Americans against the financial consequences of serious sudden illness. President Reagan signed the catastrophic health care measure into law on July 1, 1988.

Catastrophic Health Care

Under the law, to be phased in over a period of five years starting in January 1989, Medicare patients with catastrophic illnesses—those with heart disease or life-threatening cancers, for instance—were to be responsible for only the first $580 worth of each year's hospital bills. After that, the federal government would take over with unlimited free hospital care for the rest of that year. After January of 1990, Medicare patients would pay just the first $1,370 of their annual Medicare-approved doctor bills. Other physician charges approved by Medicare would be assumed by the system. Starting in 1991, 50 percent of patients' prescription drug costs were to be covered, after a $50 deductible was paid. Prescription drug coverage was set to rise to 60 percent with a $652 deductible in 1992 and to 80 percent thereafter with a deductible not specified.

The law contained other provisions. It authorized Medicare to begin paying for 150 days a year of skilled care in nursing homes—up from 100 days a year—and for thirty-eight days a year of continuous home health care—up from fifteen days a year. In addition, it required Medicaid—the federal health care program for the needy—to take over the cost of paying Medicare premiums for the elderly and disabled whose incomes fall below the poverty line but above the level that would qualify them for regular Medicaid programs. To finance the expanded Medicare program, those enrolled in it were to begin paying extra monthly premiums and surcharges.

Many of the elderly reacted to the new law with resentment. First, they were disappointed that Congress refused to allow the federal government to assume the costs of long-term care for the chronically ill of all ages. According to experts, a chronic care law, to pay for home care and nursing home care, would have done more for more Americans than the catastrophic care one ever could.

That's because chronic illness is far more common, and usually more expensive, than a catastrophic, or acute, condition. A chronic illness is one that is drawn out over a long period of time. (The word "chronic" comes from the Greek *chronos*, "time.") Parkinson's disease, a condition that slowly destroys the brain, is one chronic illness. Another is Alzheimer's, which also attacks the brain and memory and ends in senility and death. Since these and other chronic illnesses frequently strike people when they are in their fifties or sixties, victims can expect to need expert nursing care—not 150 days a year, but 365 days—for years or even decades. Such care can run to $1,000 a week or more. It's understandable that Congress refused to permit the government to take on the huge cost, but the refusal left millions of people at substantial economic risk.

Secondly, many of the elderly were outraged at the thought of paying the surcharges needed to provide for catastrophic illness coverage. They began pressing for the repeal of the new law, and late in 1989 Congress obliged by overturning it.

But federal lawmakers were also passing more popular legislation. On October 1, 1988, House and Senate leaders struck a deal, agreeing to revamp the nation's welfare system. Why, after twenty years of talking, had the U.S. Congress finally enacted a welfare reform plan?

Reasons for Reform

There were a number of reasons. One was that by the late 1980s, Congress and the country had at last come to recognize that the system in place was an outmoded one. It was a system designed for the world as it had been fifty years earlier, a system incompatible with the world as it had become.

In 1935, Congress enacted Aid to Dependent Children out of a desire to protect those members of society who seemed most vulnerable: widows, orphans, and families whose breadwinner—in those days virtually always the husband and father—had run off and deserted them. ADC and later, similar programs were, in other words, designed around the idea of the traditional family—working father, at-home mother, and children—and aimed at preserving that family by stepping in to replace its provider in the rather unusual event that he died or disappeared.

But it is no longer unusual for families to break up, and the traditional nuclear family is now hardly the norm in the United States. Divorce and remarriage, and second and third divorces and remarriages, too, are common. Many fathers, not just a few, abandon their families, and growing numbers of mothers have done the same. Single motherhood is practically a way of life for some, and unwed teenage pregnancy is widespread. Working mothers are the rule. A system built around the old-fashioned family is irrelevant in a world in which the father may never have been present, in which stepparents and children come and go, in which uneducated, unskilled children, some of them as young as twelve or thirteen, give birth to babies of their own. Any welfare system that is to function must take into account the new realities of American family life and stop trying to mimic the social structure of a vanished past. Finally coming to grips with that reality gave Congress a new basis for considering reform ideas.

Also helping the members of Congress reach agreement on welfare reform was the fact that they were finally reaching agreement on welfare itself. There was a growing consensus that it was the system not the people in the system that was largely to blame for the welfare mess. "A monstrous, consuming outrage," President Nixon had called that system in 1971. "An outrage, an absolute outrage," New York Senator Daniel Patrick Moynihan said of it in 1988.

Moynihan, chairman of the Senate Finance Committee's Social Security and Family Policy Subcommittee, was a Democrat and a liberal on social issues. Nixon was a Republican and a conservative. Yet the two, and others all along the political spectrum, were finding common language and a common ground at last. Twenty years of a maximum of argument and a minimum of action had allowed welfare to drift into such deep crisis that everyone knew genuine reform was the only way out. Members of Congress recognized, too, that if reform was to become reality, a lot of old ideas and prejudices were going to have to make way for new agreements and sweeping compromises.

Such changes didn't mean that liberals and conservatives had altered their fundamental social and political thinking overnight, but they did indicate that members of both groups had managed to give up some cherished ideas. For their part, Democrats like Senator

Moynihan had to abandon their decades-long assumption that the only way to overcome want and need was to continue on down the road of the New Deal and the War on Poverty and enact one new spending program after another. Any welfare reform package that Republicans would support would have to include strict spending curbs, they knew. It would have to include a workfare provision, too. Reluctantly, Democrats lent their support to both.

Republicans in their turn saw they would have to move away from their all-consuming concern about welfare's money costs and began thinking about its human costs, as well. One-fifth of American children were growing up in poverty, ignorance, and despair. Close to half of all homeless youngsters were getting no education. Instead of not being able to afford to help these children and their families, Republicans were now saying that the nation couldn't afford *not* to.

Why not? If the next generation cannot be educated and prepared for the workplace, the United States will face a serious labor shortage before the turn of the century, economists, including conservative economists, warn. New Jersey's Republican Governor Thomas Kean spoke to that point shortly before Congress endorsed welfare reform. Unless job-training programs were beefed up, his state would have 150,000 unfilled jobs by the mid-1990s, he estimated. "We need these people"—welfare children and their parents—"desperately in the economy," he said. Democrat Bill Clinton, governor of Arkansas, agreed. "We really don't have a person to waste in this country," he pointed out.

It was significant that the nation's governors were speaking out so bluntly about welfare issues. For it was those governors and their states who provided the final, and perhaps the most decisive, element in securing congressional agreement on reform.

When Ronald Reagan insisted upon cutting federal domestic spending, he threw much of the burden for providing relief onto the governors' shoulders. In a number of cases, the governors and their states responded with innovative workable programs. Some were

110

aimed at increasing the long-term earnings of welfare recipients, allowing them to get jobs and get out of the system, thereby saving the public money. Programs in Arkansas, Maryland, and Virginia met with special success. Welfare women with children over the age of six in those states were required to show up for job training as a condition of receiving aid. At the end of three years, the women with training were earning several hundred dollars more a year than those without it. New Jersey had experimented with workfare, too, obliging some welfare recipients to sign a contract under which they agree to get a job, take job training, or go to school. In return, the state pays for day care, health benefits, and transportation costs. In Maine, a state-sponsored job-training program was offered through private industry. Maine also helped lead the nation in setting up day care centers for working mothers.

Other states directed their attention toward different aspects of public assistance. In the mid-eighties, Massachusetts Governor Michael Dukakis announced the establishment of a child-support enforcement unit. Operating through the state's Department of Revenue—its tax-collection bureaucracy—unit members track down missing parents and force them to contribute to their children's support. Putting legal liens on property and bank accounts, assigning wages, and even arresting parents who flee the state are three methods that Bay State officials have used to force support payments. In its first year, the Massachusetts collection program allowed state officials to drop 8,000 families from the welfare rolls. If Massachusetts could accomplish that, members of the U.S. Congress asked themselves, why couldn't they? If legislators in New Jersey, Arkansas, and other states could come up with plans that succeeded in getting welfare recipients off the dole and into jobs, why couldn't Congress attempt as much?

And so Congress did—but it wasn't easy. Not only did individual Senators and Representatives disagree with one another as to exactly what sort of reform was needed and how much it should cost, the

House as a whole and the Senate as a whole also had their differences. The House, for instance, favored spending $7 billion over a five-year period; the Senate wanted to limit costs to $2.8 billion over the same length of time. The Senate was adamant in its support for a workfare provision; House members were less enthusiastic. A majority of Representatives also objected to Senate insistence upon requiring one parent in each two-parent welfare home to perform at least sixteen hours of community service each week. Still, the Representatives managed to swallow that particular objection. The community service provision "is something the House does not like, but it's the price of passing the welfare bill," said Representative Thomas J. Downey of New York. The House also agreed to the workfare element while the Senate went along with a somewhat higher price tag than it really wanted.

Even then, the compromising was not over. Not only did both houses of Congress have to agree on the reform package, Reagan had to agree too. If he refused to sign it into law, it was unlikely that Congress would pass it over his veto. Welfare reform would fail once more.

The negotiations among House, Senate, and president took three months. Finally, on September 26, 1988, they reached a successful conclusion. Within the week, the two houses had enacted identical bills. President Reagan signed the act on October 13. It was a historic moment, nearly everyone agreed. The AFDC era was over. The JOBS era was about to begin.

Jobs Opportunities and Basic Skills

JOBS stands for Jobs Opportunities and Basic Skills. The new federal welfare law requires each state to operate a JOBS program. Under them, ablebodied welfare recipients—most of whom are expected to be mothers in single-parent families—will have to work, train for a job, or go to school. Only if the recipients have children under the age of three will they be excused from this requirement, although the law permits individual states to require participation from parents with

112

children as young as a year. As for unemployed two-parent families, one adult in each must be looking for work in order to receive benefits. (This provision was set to go into effect in 1994.) Any who fail to find work must perform that sixteen weekly hours of community service, although parents in their teens or early twenties may substitute high school classes for service. There will be no increases in cash benefits under the new program, but JOBS parents may receive transportation subsidies, child-care help, and some Medicaid assistance. The subsidies and other extra help will be available for up to a year in each case, and recipients may be required to pay for them on a sliding scale.

"We have redefined the whole question of dependency," Senator Moynihan said delightedly as he saw the reform measure he had worked so hard for become law. "This is no longer to be a permanent or even extended circumstance. It is to be a transition to employment." What's more, he added, as far as single-parent families are concerned, "It is to be accompanied by child support from the absent parent."

Lawmakers expected the child-support provision to save the federal government a great deal of money. States will be told to step up their collection efforts and to withhold child-support payments from the wages of absent parents if a court so orders. The states will receive federal funds to set up computerized systems to enable them to track down delinquent parents.

The new law also seeks to help preserve families and keep them together. For the first time, the U.S. government will require all states to pay cash benefits to poor families with two parents at home. However, states that want to may limit those payments to six months out of every year. Finally, the states must concentrate most of their monetary outlay on the toughest cases—young parents without high school educations and long-term recipients, for instance. Here, too, the idea is to turn welfare dependents into men and women equipped to hold jobs that provide good wages and adequate benefits.

Will JOBS Do the Job?

Will welfare reform bring about the hoped-for transformation of the country's relief population? Some have their doubts.

Much of the doubt centers—predictably enough—around money. The reform compromise worked out between Congress and the White House set a federal spending limit of $3.34 billion over the program's first five years. That's more than the $2.8 billion the Senate wanted to spend, but a far cry from the $7 billion the House thought necessary. It's light years away from the $20 to $30 billion David Ellwood mentioned. It won't do much good to force welfare recipients to take job training courses if the courses are so poorly funded that they provide little meaningful training. Unless the courses are really worthwhile, Representative Downey points out, making recipients complete them will be "like issuing diplomas to people who didn't attend school." Others fear that the primary beneficiaries of the JOBS program may turn out to be the nation's for-profit trade schools, which are expected to enjoy a substantial increase in student enrollment.

There may be other problems. Many Americans in and out of Congress still think the community service requirement for the jobless is a poor idea. Wouldn't those sixteen hours a week be better spent looking for work or staying at home with young children? they ask.

Most controversial of all is the workfare requirement. One U.S. Representative, Augustus F. Hawkins of California, called it "slavefare." To him, it conjured up visions of nineteenth century English workhouses. Another Californian, Joanna K. Weinberg, who teaches public policy at the state university at Berkeley, also criticized this aspect of welfare reform. "Workfare is the current embodiment of the American work ethic," she wrote after completing a study of mandatory workfare. It's just another way of trying to separate the "good" poor from the "bad." Weinberg continued, " 'Good citizens' will find jobs, and the 'undeserving' will be punished."

Weinberg listed specific workfare drawbacks. Unless there is a constant supply of good, new jobs, people will be shunted off into

114

low-paying, unskilled jobs. Most such jobs provide only $400 more a year than the typical welfare grant. That amount is not much of an inducement to get off relief. What workfare tends to do, she concluded, is to "legitimize subsistence income as a permanent standard of living for some." It may remove some people from the welfare system, but that is not the same as giving them the opportunity to attain a decent way of life.

Is the workfare the way to financial independence for America's poor? Or is it merely punitive? Will JOBS means jobs—good jobs—for the nation's underclass? Can $3.34 billion—a large sum of money in itself—be stretched out over five years to provide adequately for our needy? Will welfare reform work to clear up the welfare mess? Or will the same old problems—greediness, inefficiency, muddled bureaucracy, the dependency trap—continue to plague the system? Those were just some of the welfare questions Americans were taking with them into the 1990s.

7

What Lies Ahead?

How will American welfare systems change as the country heads into the 1990s—and beyond? That change they will seems certain. The 1988 federal welfare reform act should see to that.

Other factors, too, suggest that change is on the way. Just three months after the United States got its new welfare law, it also got a new president. On January 20, 1989, George Herbert Walker Bush took the oath of office. Bush, a Republican, had served two terms as Reagan's vice-president. But although he had been a loyal member of the administration, faithfully defending its antipoverty spending cuts, *President* Bush announced at once that he would take a somewhat different tack on social issues. He particularly emphasized the contribution he expected to come from charities and volunteers.

The new tone was quickly picked up by some of Bush's choices for top government jobs. His nominee for the post of Secretary of Housing and Urban Development, former New York Representative Jack Kemp, told Senators that HUD had been woefully underfunded during the previous administration. As head of the department, he would fight for an increased federal role in the building of low-cost public housing and would work to ease what he called the "appalling problem" of homelessness. When a few months later Americans began

116

finding out about HUD corruption during the Reagan years, Kemp promised to clean up the agency mess. The new president's choice for Secretary of Defense, Representative Richard Cheney of Wyoming, backed away from some of the more expensive programs introduced by the Reagan Defense Department, vowing not to let military spending get out of hand. That promise led many to hope that the money saved might be redirected toward America's disadvantaged.

Roadblocks to Change?

But would a reduction in defense spending and an unspecified boost in federal housing efforts really do much for the nation's neediest? Many were afraid not. Bush's assumption that our social and economic problems could be solved through a combination of good will and volunteerism was, they thought, based upon his failure to take account of the seriousness of those problems.

One problem concerned the continuing federal budget deficits. In 1989, the national debt had reached a record $2.35 trillion. How could a president reduce the deficit and at the same time come up with extra money for public housing and the like? Only by raising taxes, many Americans said. But Bush had promised over and over that he would not ask Congress for any kind of a tax increase.

There was another economic problem. Business had done well during the Reagan years, but no serious economist expected the good times to last indefinitely. One warning that they would not came in October 1987, when the stock market suffered a severe drop in prices. Although followed by a quick recovery, the crash was a reminder that good times are invariably followed by bad.

Yet other problems were social: stubborn unemployment among certain groups and in certain parts of the country; the breakdown of the family and a growing number of single-parent homes; and high numbers of teenage pregnancies. We have seen throughout this book the burden such problems have placed upon welfare systems.

Finally, and most ominous, was the fact that the gap between rich and poor was widening. According to figures from the U.S. Census Bureau and the Economic Policy Institute, a Washington, D.C., research center, the average family income of the poorest one-fifth of Americans declined by 10.9 percent between 1979 and 1986. The average income of the wealthiest one-fifth of families went up by 13.8 percent over the same years. Many expect that trend to continue, deepening poverty and threatening social unrest.

Signs of Hope

Is there then no hope for the future? Of course not. Some people may disagree with some of President Bush's policies or believe he underestimated the severity of the nation's problems, but few doubted the earnestness of his desire to see Americans do more for one another. And hopes were still high that welfare reform would bring real, positive changes.

There were other signs of hope as well. One was a new attention being paid to the problems of the poor by large foundations. In 1989, the Rockefeller Foundation, which had previously fought hunger and disease in faraway parts of the world, decided to redirect its attention closer to home. Foundation officials announced a new multi-million dollar program aimed at understanding America's underclass, the people "government and everyone wants to forget," as the group's president, Peter C. Goldmark, put it. Another innovative venture into social service came from the $400 million Annie E. Casey Foundation. In 1987, that foundation, named in honor of the mother of its founder—who was also the founder of United Parcel Service—announced that it was putting $50 million into a program for children at risk. Under the program, $10-million grants would be offered to each of five cities that came up with pioneering plans to assist uneducated, jobless, or pregnant teens. Another $50 million would go toward working for changes in juvenile welfare policies.

The most hopeful sign of all, however, was what seemed to be a new concern for the unfortunate on the part of Americans in general.

A 1989 poll showed that 75 percent of those questioned thought government at all levels had failed to do enough for the homeless throughout the 1980s. That was up from the 46 percent who felt that way in 1986. Over half of those polled in 1989 said they would be willing to pay higher taxes to help end homelessness.

Concern for the homeless was more than just a matter of talk. In 1988, Mayor Edward Koch told New Yorkers that the city's policy of housing the homeless in welfare hotels would be phased out by July 1990. Families in the decaying structures would be assigned to apartments. Among the first hotels to be shut down was the Martinique, and officials suggested that the Prince George might be next on the list.

The Prince George. That was the wretched place where the Gonzalezes—Miguel, Kissey, and Nancy—had been living since 1987. How happy the three must have been at the prospect of a real home of their own. How they must have celebrated this landmark event in one American family's struggle to escape its world of welfare.

Further Reading

BOOKS

Bender, David L., *The Welfare State: Opposing Viewpoints*, St. Paul, MN: Greenhaven Press, 1982.

Buckley, William F., Jr., *Four Reforms: A Program for the 70s*, NY: G. P. Putnam's Sons, 1973.

Ellwood, David T., *Poor Support: Poverty in the American Family*, NY: Basic Books, 1988.

Frazer, Derek, *The Evolution of the British Welfare State: A History of Social Policy since the Industrial Revolution*, NY: Harper & Row Publishers, Inc., 1973.

Furniss, Norman and Timothy Tilton, *The Case for the Welfare State: From Social Security to Social Equality*, Bloomington, IN: Indiana University Press, 1977.

Goldman, Eric F., *The Tragedy of Lyndon Johnson*, NY: Alfred A. Knopf, 1969.

Harrington, Michael, *The New American Poverty*, NY: Holt, Rinehart and Winston, 1984.

———. *The Other America: Poverty in the United States*, NY: The Macmillan Company, 1962.

Hazlitt, Henry, *The Conquest of Poverty*, New Rochelle, NY: Arlington House, 1973.

Hyde, Margaret O., *The Homeless: Profiling the Problem*, Hillside, NJ: Enslow Publishers, 1989.

Jaffe, Natalie, *Public Welfare: Facts, Myths, and Prospects*, NY: Public Affairs Pamphlets, 1977.

Kozol, Jonathan, *Rachel and Her Children: Homeless Families in America*, NY: Crown Publishers, 1988.

Longmate, Norman, *The Workhouse*, NY: St. Martin's Press, 1974.

Mandell, Betty Reid, ed., *Welfare in America: Controlling the "Dangerous Classes,"* Englewood Cliffs, NJ: Prentice-Hall, Inc., 1975.

Nielsen, Waldemar A., *The Golden Donors: A New Anatomy of the Great Foundations*, New York: E.P. Dutton, 1985.

Piven, Frances Fox and Richard A. Cloward, *Poor People's Movements: Why They Succeed, How They Fall*, NY: Pantheon Books, 1977.

Schwartz-Nobel, Loretta, *Starving in the Shadow of Plenty,* NY: G.P. Putnam's Sons, 1981.

Thurow, Lester C., *Poverty and Discrimination,* Washington, D.C.: The Brookings Institution, 1969.

Trecker, Harleigh B., ed., *Goals for Social Welfare 1973-1993: An Overview of the Next Two Decades*, New York: Association Press, 1973.

Wise, Winifred E., *Jane Addams of Hull-House*, New York: Harcourt, Brace and Company, 1935.

PERIODICALS

Barbanel, Josh. "For Welfare Mothers, New Possibilities." *The New York Times*, July 7, 1988.

———. "Joyce Brown Is Hospitalized After Collapsing." *The New York Times,* May 11, 1988.

———. "Koch Plan Would Speed Welfare Hotels' Closing." *The New York Times*, July 15, 1988.

———. "Welfare Rules Said to Add to Homeless." *The New York Times,* May 14, 1987.

———. "Welfare Excesses Fall but Improper Removals Rise." *The New York Times*, September 17, 1987.

Bernstein, Richard. "King's Dream: America Still Haunted by Problems of Black Poor." *The New York Times*, January 17, 1988.

Brozan, Nadine. "Former Wives: A Legion of the Needy." *The New York Times*, July 19, 1987.

"Bush Signs a Bill Increasing the Minimum Wage to $4.25." *The New York Times*, November 19, 1989.

Carmody, Deirdre. "Head Start Gets Credit For Rise in Scores." *The New York Times,* September 21, 1988.

Chavez, Lydia. "Welfare Hotel Children: Tomorrow's Poor." *The New York Times*, July 16, 1987.

"Children of Transients Are Denied Schooling." *The New York Times,* March 17, 1987.

Dow, George. "Nobleboro History." *The Lincoln County News*, September 2, 1987.

Duncan, Greg J., Martha S. Hill, Saul D. Hoffman. "Welfare Dependence Within and Across Generations." *Science,* Vol. 239, 29 January 1988.

Ellwood, David T. "From welfare reform to replacing welfare." *The Boston Globe*, July 31, 1988.

Erlanger, Steven. " 'State of Art' Computers Delay Welfare Benefits in New York." *The New York Times*, December 26, 1987.

Freedman, Samuel G. "At Welfare Hotel, a Grant for Organizers Gives Hope." *The New York Times*, July 15, 1987.

Gay, Lance. "Congress says welfare crackdown hurts poor." *Kennebec Journal*, August 24, 1987.

Gross, Jane. "For a Teen-Age Mother, a Job and Guidance." *The New York Times*, October 22, 1987.

Hale, Karlene K. "Laurie looks forward to a future without welfare." *Kennebec Journal,* December 26, 1987.

Hey, Robert P. "Big cities are losing the poverty battle." *The Christian Science Monitor*, December 17, 1987.

———. "New tack in welfare reform." *The Christian Science Monitor,* June 20, 1988.

———. "Workfare benefits modest but lasting." *The Christian Science Monitor*, June 22, 1988.

"Hospitals Found to Overbill Medicare by $2 Billion a Year." *The New York Times*, January 18, 1988.

"Huge Medicare Fraud Found." *The New York Times*, May 21, 1988.

Johnson, Julie. "Tough Words to Translate: 'Kinder and Gentler.'" *The New York Times*, January 25, 1989.

Johnson, Kirk. "The Taking of Car No. 4776: Homeless Men Find a Haven." *The New York Times,* May 11, 1988.

Kilborn, Peter T. "The Temptations of the Social Security Surplus." *The New York Times*, November 27, 1988.

Koch, Edward I. "Welfare Isn't A Way Of Life." *The New York Times*, March 4, 1988.

LaFranchi, Howard. "Coming to the rescue of children growing up in poverty." *The Christian Science Monitor*, July 15, 1987.

———. "Public aid in stricken oil patch." *The Christian Science Monitor,* September 1, 1987.

———. "The 'new poor' in the oil patch." *The Christian Science Monitor,* August 31, 1987.

Lambert, Bruce. "New York Faulted on Tuberculosis." *The New York Times,* January 24, 1988.

Layfield, Denise. "Portland jail is 'home' for some in winter." *Kennebec Journal,* November 19, 1987.

Lee, Susan and Mary Beth Grover. "Social Security Faces a $600 Billion Question." *The New York Times,* July 23, 1989.

Lewin, Tamar. "Nation's Homeless Veterans Battle a New Foe: Defeatism." *The New York Times,* December 30, 1987.

Lohr, Steve. "British Health Service Faces a Crisis in Funds and Delays." *The New York Times,* August 7, 1988.

Loth, Renee. "Child-support collections up 30 percent, state reports." *The Boston Globe,* July 3, 1988.

Louie, Elaine. "At Library, a Room for the Homeless." *The New York Times,* January 19, 1988.

McBride, Nicholas C. "Not only do rich get richer, they vote more, too." *The Christian Science Monitor,* May 5, 1988.

Mitgang, Lee. "'Latchkey children' take refuge in library stacks." *Kennebec Journal,* April 6, 1988.

Morley, Jefferson. "The New Anti-Poverty Debate." *The Nation,* February 13, 1988.

"Needlessly Harsh on Student Loans." *The New York Times,* April 30, 1988.

Noble, Kenneth B. "Quayle Is Proud, and Others Skeptical, of Job Plan." *The New York Times,* September 4, 1988.

O'Hare, William. "Separating Welfare Fact From Fiction." *The Wall Street Journal,* December 14, 1987.

Pear, Robert. "20% of Claims For Medicare Termed Faulty." *The New York Times,* February 11, 1988.

———. "U.S. Pensions Found to Lift Many of Poor." *The New York Times,* December 28, 1988.

Perlez, Jane. "Thousands of Pupils Living in Hotels Skip School in New York." *The New York Times,* November 12, 1987.

"Providing for the poor." *The Christian Science Monitor,* January 13, 1988.

Rimer, Sara. "In Suburb, Poor People in Despair at a Motel." *The New York Times,* April 5, 1988.

Riordan, Teresa. "Housekeeping at HUD." *Common Cause Magazine,* March/April 1987.

Roberts, Sam. "For Homeless, Struggles Include Getting to School." *The New York Times,* April 23, 1987.

————. "Old Hotel Does Import Business in the Homeless. *The New York Times,* April 28, 1988.

Rosenbaum, David E. "Celebrating, as It Were, Anniversary on Poverty." *The New York Times*, October 7, 1987.

"Runaways of the 80's: Victims Of Abuse." *The New York Times*, January 11, 1988.

Schmidt, William E. "The Depression Deepens in the Mountain States." *The New York Times,* June 26, 1988.

Schneider, Keith. "Louisiana Sugar Industry Thrives Amid Job Loss." *The New York Times,* June 3, 1988.

————. "New Product on Farms in Midwest: Hunger." *The New York Times,* September 29, 1987.

Scruggs, Roberta. "Masks: A prison reformer becomes a prisoner." *The Maine Times*, July 17, 1987.

Shenon, Philip. "Documents Show Active Pierce Role on Fund Requests." *The New York Times,* July 23, 1989.

————. "H.U.D. Dropping Washington Office's Chief and 3 Staff Members." *The New York Times*, July 22, 1989.

Silk, Leonard. "Now, to Figure Why the Poor Get Poorer." *The New York Times*, December 18, 1988.

Steese, Ellen. "Home is where the hotel is..." *The Christian Science Monitor,* May 5, 1988.

————. "Unlocking the welfare trap." *The Christian Science Monitor*, July 20, 1987.

Stevens, William K. "Some Preliminary Results in the Rush From Welfare to Work." *The New York Times,* August 21, 1988.

————. "The Welfare Consensus." *The New York Times,* June 22, 1988.

————. "Welfare Bill: Historic Scope but a Gradual Impact." *The New York Times*, October 2, 1988.

"Study Calls U.S. a Country Deeper in Debt to Minorities." *The New York Times*, May 24, 1988.

"Study says families make up one-third of homeless." *The Christian Science Monitor*, May 11, 1987.

Teltsch, Kathleen. "Charity to Focus on Underclass." *The New York Times,* January 22, 1989.

————. "Corporate Pressures Slowing Gifts to Charity." *The New York Times*, June 8, 1987.

————. "From a Foundation, $100 Million for Children." *The New York Times,* November 3, 1987.

————. "Increase in Charitable Donations in '87 Was Lowest in 12 Years." *The New York Times,* June 26, 1988.

Thomas, Owen. "Harvard professor champions a bolder plan for welfare reform." *The Christian Science Monitor,* June 23, 1988.

Tolchin, Martin. "Congress Leaders and White House Agree on Welfare." *The New York Times,* September 27, 1988.

————. "Efforts to Revamp Welfare System Face Steep Hurdles in Congress." *The New York Times*, June 29, 1988.

————. "Federal Aid for Destitute Reaching Just Half of Those Eligible." *The New York Times,* May 10, 1988.

————. "For Many, Help Is Near on Health Costs." *The New York Times,* May 31, 1988.

————. "Moynihan Seeking to Stand System on Its Head." *The New York Times,* June 13, 1988.

————. "Paradox of Reagan Budgets Hints Contradiction in Legacy." *The New York Times,* February 16, 1988.

————. "Welfare Changes Endangered, Governors Say." *The New York Times*, May 21, 1989.

Toner, Robin. "Americans Favor Aid for Homeless." *The New York Times,* January 22, 1989.

"Transcript of Bush's Inaugural Address: 'Nation Stands Ready to Push On.'" *The New York Times,* January 21, 1989.

United States Department of Agriculture, Food and Nutrition Service. "Food Stamp Program: A Guide for Retailers." Program Aid No. 1221, 1983.

————. "Food Stamp Program: Cashier Training Manual." Program Aid No. 1176, 1985.

"Welfare's Day Care Corollary." *The New York Times*, November 14, 1987.

Weinberg, Joanna K. "Workfare—It Isn't Work, It Isn't Fair." *The New York Times*, August 19, 1988.

Wicker, Tom. "Always With Us." *The New York Times,* November 19, 1987.

Wycliff, Don. "Q & A: William Julius Wilson, How the Urban Poor Got Poorer." *The New York Times*, November 29, 1987.

Index